Y0-BRG-454

CLASSIC
American
BARBECUE

Copyright © 1993
Cookbook Publishers, Inc.
Olathe, Kansas 66061

All rights reserved. No part of this publication may be reproduced or transmitted in any form by any means, electronic or mechanical, including photocopy, recording, or any information storage or retrieval system, without permission in writing from the publishers, except by a reviewer who wishes to quote brief passages in connection with a review written for inclusion in a magazine, newspaper, or broadcast.

Printed in the USA

ISBN #0-934474-66-4

TABLE OF CONTENTS

FAVORITE RECIPES
FROM MY COOKBOOK

Recipe Name	Page Number

GRILLING BASICS

The last word in eating is a nice thick grilled steak! People receive a satisfied feeling of great dining with a steak's mouth-watering aroma, plus its outstanding flavor, tenderness and juiciness.

How people should like a steak cooked is a point people debate. A delightful book, *The First Really Important Survey of American Habits*, gives us some insights into America's steak-eating habits. Its authors found that 59% of Americans like their steaks cooked medium, 26% liked them rare, and only 15% wanted them well-done.

Regardless of how people like the center of their steak, burger, or chop, they prefer seared meats with lightly charred crusts. Why? These meats have a more intense caramelized flavor with greater aroma. People may want them cooked well-done, but they still want them juicy. This presents a problem to the cook-out cook. Before we move on to grilling a steak, burger, or a chop, let's have a look at some basic grilling ideas.

Grilling's Effect On Flavor

Grilling's hot dry air (400°F. up to 550°F.) sears meat and evaporates the water from its juices. This leaves a browned caramelized outside crust. Using these higher temperatures, meat needs only 3 to 4 minutes of searing on its serve side to produce this attractive flavorful crust. This develops grilled foods' superb aromas. These temperatures and time brown meat to a depth of $1/32$ to $1/16$" below meat's surfaces. You lower the heat to finish grilling after searing thicker pieces.

To produce this browned crust when grilling thinner cuts ($1/2$" thick or less) of meat and fish presents a problem. If you want a browned outside, you overcook the meat's center easily. These searing temperatures destroy much of the coating of herbs and seasonings (dry rubs or marinades) on the meat's surfaces. So you need to apply extra seasonings if you want flavors to come through. With bone-in chicken, use 350°F. up to 400°F. and grill for a longer time to develop its crust and cook it to the desired doneness.

Grilling's Effect On Juiciness

You need to retain all of your meat's natural juices! You may want to add to their juices by using a tasty baste or marinade. You need a baste which contains some vegetable oil for lean cuts of meat to help them retain juiciness. You grill meat only until the center is just barely done to your liking. For the best juicy centers, meat's cooked centers range from 130°F. to 160°F. for beef and lamb, 150°F. to 160°F. for pork, 165°F. for poultry, and 135°F to 140°F. for most fish. Beyond these temperatures, you dry out foods unnecessarily. When you grill poultry or even fatter red meat cuts to 165°F. and beyond you should baste them to keep them juicy.

Grilling's Effect On Tenderness

Grilling toughens tender meat if it is cooked too long. You want to retain all of the meat's natural tenderness. With grilling, you can start with (1) a natural tender cut of meat, (2) a tenderized tougher cut, or (3) ground meats. When you grill slightly tougher cuts of meat above a rare 140°F., their tougher connective tissues (collagen) start to convert to tender gelatin. However, the best interior doneness temperature of very tender cuts of red meats is 140°F., but the meats will be rare and red. Your best doneness temperature is 145°F. to 150°F. (a pink color) for slightly tougher cuts of meat.

Rethink Grilling

With the "Healthy Heart" push to eat less meat, thinner meat cuts may work better for some people. Grilling a steak or chop with (1) full-flavored browned crusty outside, (2) juicy rare, or medium rare or medium center -- may take some re-thinking of grilling techniques. Few people praise dried-out, tough grilled meats.

Solutions for Grilling Problems

(1) Start with a hot grill fire 450°F. to 550°F. for *Quick Grilling*. Paint the hot grid with cold vegetable oil to reduce sticking of the meat to the grid. Then grill immediately.

(2) Use intermittent flame-ups for the first 3 to 4 minutes on each side to sear and lightly char meats for a fuller flavor.

(3) Blot meat free of moisture or liquids just before you start to grill, if you can. Moisture slows down the browning effect. If part of your seasoning is a liquid (Worcestershire sauce, etc.), you can't blot it.

(4) Use a Browning Rub if needed.

The weight of a cut of meat does not determine the grilling time -- a 2 pound top sirloin steak may be 2" thick or 1" thick. The grilling time for a 1-inch-thick cut of meat will be about 60% of the time compared with 2-inch-thick cut of meat. *One Big Grilling Rule: Generally, meat 1" thick will cook to 140°F. (rare beef or lamb) in 8 to 10 minutes using a medium hot fire.*

With all direct grilling the top of the food grid or rack will have hot and cool spots. You move thin foods to the outside edges of the fire. Place longer-grilled foods in the center of the grid.

Different Thicknesses

(1) For ½-inch-thick meats grilled to a rare or medium rare center, apply the Browning Rub first. Then freeze the meats on a cookie sheet and grill them nearly frozen.

(2) For ¾-inch-thick meats, start with semi-thawed meats using the Browning Rub.

(3) For 1-inch-thick meats, start with cold meats from the refrigerator, then grill.

(4) For 1½-inch to 2-inch-thick meats, bring to room temperature.

(5) Grill all thicker meats with a medium hot fire until seared, then grill on low to cook the center.

Some cookbooks give recommendations for you to place meat and chicken 6 inches above the heat source and fish 4 to 6 inches. This distance could be 3 inches on a very slow fire for chicken or 3 inches for a hot fire when searing a steak. Whatever the meat's distance from the fire, you need to know the grid's cooking temperature.

Measuring Grilling Temperatures

FOR GAS, CHARCOAL, AND ELECTRIC GRILLS: The best method for knowing grilling temperatures is an inexpensive oven thermometer which measures up to 600°F. SECRETS' Hand/Palm heat-sensing method substitutes accurately enough for a thermometer when grilling at higher temperatures. Use an oven or candy thermometer when your cooking temperatures need to be below 300°F.

Hand/Palm Heat-Sensing System

This system consists of holding your palm, at its *normal* body temperature, one inch above the cooking grid level and saying "1001" up to "1006". You hold this position and count before the fire forces your hand away. Each one of these "1001s" through "1006" equals one second.

You'll receive a false reading if your hand has been holding a cold drink -- or if you've just checked the fire. You'll count to "1006" with the heated palm and "1002" with the cold drink palm, both with the same 350°F. LOW fire.

SPECIFIC READINGS: Saying "1001" up to "1002" equals a very high (550°F. to 700°F.) fire; saying "1001" up to "1003" equals a medium hot or "high" (500°F.) fire; saying "1001" up to "1005" equals a low (350°F.) fire; "1006" equals a very low and slow (300°F.) grilling fire.

Safe Grilling: Using Charcoal, Gas, or Electric

(1) Always keep a fire extinguisher handy.

(2) Keep all types of grills uncovered while starting the fire. Don't cover a charcoal fire until all the lighter fluid has been burned off.

(3) Do not wear loose-hanging clothes, or use clothing or hot pads with a fringe when working over the fire.

(4) Use long-handled tools for basting and turning foods.

(5) Keep children away from hot grills.

(6) Keep grill 5 feet away from the building's wooden overhang.

(7) Use the grill's cover (hood, lid) to put out fat fires of charcoal grills, or help control them (gas grills).

(8) Keep a water bottle (clean detergent bottle with a pouring cap) next to the grill for pouring a quick short stream of water on a fat fire. Water spritzers can chase fat fires. However, intermittent flame-ups produce the lightly-charred flavor of excellent grilled foods.

(9) If you grill indoors, use the fireplace for ventilating smoke.

(10) To clean the grid, heat for five minutes and brush with a brass wire brush or nylon pad to reduce meat sticking.

(11) Use tongs to turn meats. Use a wide-tined fork to gently lift under ground meat patties after grilling 2 to 3 minutes, which helps with sticking.

(12) Heat the grid hot to produce grill marks. Then brush with cold vegetable oil. Then place the meat on the grill.

Grilling's Two Types

Grilling is divided into two types: indirect and direct. Direct grilling places food directly over the "fire", which may be gas, charcoal, or electric. The "fire's" dry heat cooks the food above it on the grill's grid. This direct grilling method works best when cooking meats with nearly equal thickness and which lay flat on the grid. You use direct grilling to cook steaks, burgers, chops, chicken, turkey, or rabbit pieces, whole fish, fish fillets, and sausages. It caramelizes, lightly smokes and lightly chars the food, and gives it a browned grill-marked appearance. With direct grilling, the grill's cover may be closed or open or a combination of the two.

Meats lying on the grids receive the results of the fire's direct heat with the cover closed. The top of the meat is heated by indirect hot air flowing over it and will be 100°F. up to 150°F. cooler. Direct-grilled meats can be *Quick Grilled* -- cooked in 5 up to 20 minutes, or *Slow Grilled* in 30 to 60 minutes using lower temperatures. You do most home grilling with the grill's cover closed. This increases the grid's temperature as much as 75°F. to 150°F.

"Grilling Basics", from Barbecuing and Sausage-Making SECRETS, is used courtesy of Charlie and Ruthie Knote, authors of the "most complete barbecuing reference cookbook." 276 pages. Culinary Institute of Smoke-Cooking, P.O. Box 163, Cape Girardeau, Missouri 63701.

GRILLING GUIDE
For Charcoal or Gas or Electric Grills

Medium Hot Fire = 450° to 500°F.
Medium Fire = 350° to 400°F.

Type of Food	Meat Cut or Portion	Meat Thickness	Fire Temp.	APPROXIMATE Total Grilling Time in Minutes		
				Rare 140°F.	Medium 155°F. - 160°F.	Well Done 165°F. - 170°F.
Burgers	Beef, Pork, Lamb, or Chicken	½ inch	Med. Hot	7 - 9	9 - 11	11 - 14
		¾ inch	Med. Hot	8 - 11	11 - 13	11 - 17
Beef Steak	Porterhouse, T-Bone, Top Sirloin	¾ inch	Med. Hot	9 - 12	12 - 13	15 - 18
		1 inch	Med. Hot	9 - 12	12 - 16	16 - 20
		1½ inches	Med. Hot/ drop to Med.	15 - 18	19 - 24	12 - 26
Pork	Loin & Rib Chops Pork Steak or Blade	1 inch	Med.	XXXX	14 - 18	19 - 24*
		1¼ inches	Med.	XXXX	16 - 20	22 - 27*
		¾ inch	Med.	XXXX	12 - 16	15 - 20*
Lamb	Rib Chops	1 inch	Med. Hot	9 - 12	12 - 16	16 - 20
		1½ inches	Med. Hot	15 - 18	19 - 24	21 - 26
	Leg Steaks or Chops	1 inch	Med. Hot	9 - 12	12 - 16	16 - 20
	Shoulder Chops	1 inch	Med. Hot	9 - 12	12 - 16	16 - 20
Chicken	Fryer Pieces, Larger Legs, Thighs, Breasts-Bone in		Med.	XXXX	XXXX	30 - 50
	Breasts Deboned Skin Off	5-8 oz. each	Med. Hot.	XXXX	XXXX	8 - 12

				Fish and Seafood		
				135°-155°F.		
Fish	Whole Dressed	1 inch	Med. Hot	8 - 10		
	Whole Dressed	1½ inches	Med. Hot	11 - 15		
	Fillets	½ inch	Med. Hot	5 - 7		
		1 inch	Med. Hot	7 - 9		
Seafood	Shrimp, Shell on	Med.	Med. Hot	4 - 7		
	Scallops	Sea 1-1½ inches	Med. Hot	7 - 10		
		Bay ½ inch	Med. Hot	5 - 8		

* Cooked Done

Comparative "Cook-Out" Methods

Raw Meat Types	Meat Thickness	Cooking Method	Grill/Smoker Temperatures	Cooking Time	Equipment Ease of Use Rating (1)	COVER: Use Open or Closed	Smoke Wood Flavoring Ability (2)	Special Instructions
Fish Fillets, Hamburger, 2-inch Steaks	1/4 inch to 2 inches	Quick Grilling	600°F. down to 300°F.	3 min. to 25 min.	GRILL 1. Gas 2. Charcoal 3. Electric	Open and/or Closed	None to Very Light	Intermittent flame & sear "outside" on HIGH; then cook center on LOW.
Turkey Breast, Brisket, Chicken, Pork Roast	2 inches to 5 inches	Slow Grilling (Rotisserie)	400°F. down to 200°F.	30 min. to 6 hr.	GRILL 1. Gas 2. Charcoal 3. Electric	Open and/or Closed	Light to Heavy	Direct Heat: Indirect low heat. Use drip pan. Add smoke wood system.
Smoked Cornish Hens, 16 lb. Shoulder, 20 lb. Turkey	1 inch to 5 inches	Water Smoker Cooking	300°F. down to 175°F.	2 hr. to 12 hr.	WATER SMOKER 1. Electric 2. Gas 3. Charcoal	Closed	Light to Very Heavy	Use water smoker or kettle grill with water pan.
Smoked Fish Filets, Sausages, Pork Loin	1/2 inch to 5 inches	Dry Smoke-Cooking	300°F. down to 175°F.	30 min. to 1 1/2 hr.	WATER SMOKER 1. With dry water pan	Closed	Light to Very Heavy	Use sawdust in smoker's dry water pan.
Smoked Pork Ribs, Whole Hogs, Brisket	1/2" inch to 6 inches	Contest Barbecuing (The Pro's)	275°F. down to 175°F.	5 hr. to 24 hr.	CUSTOM BUILT COOKER 1. Charcoal 2. Wood	Closed	Light to Very Heavy	Professional BBQ Contests. See Index
Smoking Cured Bacon, Sausage, Ham, Whole Fish	1/2 inch to 6 inches	Cold Smoking	85°F. up to 120°F.	1 hr. to 24 hr.	WATER SMOKER Charcoal or Electric (Limit Briquette Numbers)	Closed	Light to Heavy	Smoke flavoring only; doesn't cook food. Brine foods to stop bacterial growth.

(1) Ease of Use Rating Consists of: (A) Getting the equipment ready to cook, (B) Cleaning up after cooking, (C) Cooking in cold or hot weather. *Quick Grilled foods'* smoke flavor comes from

(2) Smoke Wood Flavor Ability: Smoke wood flavoring takes more than 10 to 30 minutes exposure time. *Quick Grilled foods'* smoke flavor comes from fat droplets that vaporize from the juice dripping onto the hot "rocks" in the grill's fire box.

8   Notes

BEEF

LEAN AND JUICY "BURGERS"

1½ lb. lean ground beef
  (chuck grade)
1 Tbsp. cornstarch
3 oz. water
6 Tbsp. Blue cheese (or
  American process) ,
1 tsp. bouillon granules or
  1 cube
1 tsp. salt
Vegetable oil
1 Tbsp. Worcestershire
  sauce
3 Tbsp. instant minced
  onions
Lemon pepper seasoning
  (optional)

Dissolve the bouillon in the water, then add salt, Worcestershire, minced onions, and cornstarch. Stir liquid to dissolve and mix. Please use the salt along with the water; it dissolves some of the meat's protein which makes a sticky "paste."(This "paste" holds the lean ground beef without packing.) Lightly form 12 patties about ¼ inch thick -- you "stick" the meat together without pressure. Place one tablespoon of Blue cheese on bottom patties, then cover with the top patties, and seal and smooth out edges completely. Baste the bottom of the burger with oil to help prevent sticking.

Place the pre-formed burgers on the heated, oiled grid and grill for 2 minutes using a medium hot fire. Using a long handled large 2 tined fork, straddle the grid wires underneath the front edge of each burger and lift gently. Lifting eliminates some of the sticking of the ground meat particles to the grids. Sticking causes crumbling of the burgers. Grill the burger for 1 to 2 minutes more, until firmed up, before turning with a long handled pancake turner. The burgers' turned side should be browned with nice grill marks, so you serve this side up. If desired, sprinkle them with lemon pepper seasoning lightly after turning.

Next, you start checking the turned burgers for "doneness" using the finger test. Cover your index finger with a thick cloth; gently push on the edge of the burger. It will be much firmer than the very soft middle at the rare stage. The longer you cook the burgers, the more their centers firm up from soft to spongy for medium rare to springy and finally to very firm for very well done.

- From Barbecuing & Sausage Making SECRETS

TORTILLA BURGERS

1 lb. ground beef
½ c. refried beans
¼ c. chopped green
  chilies
¼ c. chopped onions
1 Tbsp. snipped parsley
6 seven-inch flour tortillas
Taco sauce

Mix all ingredients except tortillas and taco sauce. Shape mixture into 6 oval patties, each about 4 inches long and 3 inches wide.

Grill patties about 4 inches from medium coals, turning once, until desired doneness, 5 to 7 minutes on each side for medium. Wrap tortillas in aluminum foil. Heat on grill until warm, 4 to 6 minutes. Serve patties in tortillas with taco sauce. Garnish with chopped tomato, more snipped parsley and dairy sour cream, if desired. Serves 6.

CORNBURGERS

1 lb. ground beef
3 Tbsp. pine nuts
Salt to taste
⅓ c. canned corn,
 drained
4 tsp. chili sauce
¼ c. blue cheese,
 crumbled

Combine the beef, pine nuts, and salt in a bowl. Shape meat into 10 or 12 thin patties; set aside.

Put corn, chili sauce, and blue cheese in a small bowl; mix well. Put 1 heaping tablespoon of the corn mixture in the center of each of 5 or 6 patties. Then, cover each with a second patty. Pinch the edges of the meat together to seal in the filling.

Grill the patties over medium heat, turning once. Allow 5 to 20 minutes for rare- to medium-done burgers. Makes 5 to 6.

FILLED HAMBURGERS

1½ lb. ground beef
¼ c. dry bread crumbs
2 Tbsp. water
1 Tbsp. Worcestershire
 sauce
½ tsp. salt
¼ tsp. pepper
1 egg
Fillings*

Mix all ingredients except Fillings. Shape mixture into 12 patties, each about 4 inches in diameter. Top each of 6 patties with one of the Fillings, spreading to within ½ inch of edge; top with a remaining patty and seal edge firmly.

Grill patties about 4 inches from medium coals, turning once, until desired doneness, 5 to 7 minutes on each side for medium. Serve in split hamburger buns, if desired.

*Fillings: 1 tablespoon finely chopped onion, 1 tablespoon chopped tomato, 1 tablespoon shredded Cheddar cheese or 1 to 2 teaspoons prepared horseradish. Serves 6.

JUMBO BURGER

2 lb. ground round
2 tsp. salt
Dash of pepper
2 tsp. minced onion

In a small bowl, combine the beef with the salt, pepper, and minced onion. Shape meat into 8 large, thin patties. Mound ¼ cup of your favorite stuffing mixture in the center of one patty. Top with second patty; pinch edges of meat together to seal in mixture. Grill over medium heat, turning once. A Jumbo Burger grilled 3 inches from the hot briquettes will take about 15 minutes.

HAMBURGERS SUPREME

2 Tbsp. onion, chopped
2 Tbsp. water
1 lb. ground beef
1 egg
¼ c. ketchup
⅓ c. fine dry bread
   crumbs
2 Tbsp. mustard pickle,
   finely chopped
1 Tbsp. Worcestershire
   sauce
1 tsp. salt
¼ tsp. pepper

Mix all ingredients. Shape mixture into 6 patties; chill thoroughly. Grill 4 inches from hot coals for 6 minutes on each side. Serve in toasted hamburger buns, if desired. Yields 6 burgers.

TACO BURGERS

1⅓ lb. ground chuck
¼ c. crushed tortilla
   chips
2 Tbsp. bottled taco sauce
1 tsp. salt
½ tsp. pepper, freshly
   ground
4 cornmeal or other
   hamburger buns
Optional: sliced pickled
   jalapeno peppers,
   shredded Cheddar
   cheese, chopped
   scallions, sliced
   tomatoes, shredded
   iceberg lettuce,
   additional taco sauce

Prepare a hot fire. In a medium bowl, working as quickly and gently as possible, mix ground beef with crushed tortilla chips, taco sauce, salt, and pepper. Divide mixture into quarters and lightly form into 4 patties ¾ to 1 inch thick.

Place patties on an oiled grill set 4 to 6 inches from coals. Grill, turning once, until outside is well browned and inside is slightly charred but still pink and juicy, about 8 to 12 minutes for rare to medium rare, or longer if desired.

Meanwhile, open buns and toast on sides of grill until warm and lightly browned. Place cooked burgers in buns and garnish to taste.

BACON AND CHEESE BURGERS

1⅓ lb. ground chuck
1½ tsp. salt
½ tsp. pepper, freshly
  ground
4 to 8 slices cooked
  bacon
4 slices cheese (Swiss,
  Cheddar, or American)
4 hamburger buns, onion
  rolls, or other bread
Optional: Mustard,
  ketchup, mayonnaise,
  sliced sweet onion or
  grilled onion slices,
  pickles or pickle relish,
  sliced tomatoes, lettuce
  leaves

Prepare a hot fire. In a medium bowl, working as quickly and gently as possible, mix ground beef with salt and pepper. Divide mixture into quarters and lightly form into 4 patties ¾ to 1 inch thick.

Place patties on an oiled grill over hot coals. Grill, turning once, until outside is well browned but inside is still pink and juicy, about 8 to 12 minutes for rare to medium rare, or longer if desired. Just before removing burgers from grill, top each with 1 or 2 slices of bacon and a slice of cheese.

Open buns and toast on sides of grill until warm and lightly browned. Placed cooked burgers in buns and garnish to taste.

MARINATED CHAR-BROILED BEEF

½ c. soy sauce
3 Tbsp. honey
¼ c. cider vinegar
1 Tbsp. garlic powder
1 Tbsp. ginger
1½ c. vegetable oil
2 green onions, finely
  chopped
1 round steak, 2" thick

Blend first 7 ingredients for marinade. Pour marinade on steak; cover and marinate 4 hours. Turn steak once each hour.

Drain off marinade and grill steak on outdoor grill for 15 minutes on each side (less time for very rare).Remove from grill; let stand 10 minutes before carving. Slice diagonally across the grain, as thin as possible. Serves 8-10.

GRILLED RIB STEAKS WITH ROQUEFORT BUTTER

8 beef rib steaks, 1 inch
  thick
3 Tbsp. olive oil
1 tsp. salt
¼ tsp. pepper, freshly
  ground
8 Tbsp. unsalted butter,
  softened
½ c. Roquefort cheese,
  crumbled
Dash of cayenne
1½ tsp. minced parsley

Prepare a hot fire. Rub steaks with oil and season with salt and pepper. In a food processor or blender, combine butter, cheese, cayenne, and parsley. Process until well blended. (Roquefort butter can be refrigerated up to 3 days.)

When coals are hot, place steaks on an oiled grill and cook, turning occasionally, until well browned outside and still pink and juicy inside, about 8 to 12 minutes. Top each steak with a dollop of Roquefort butter.

MARINATED GRILLED FLANK STEAK

Juice of 1 lemon
½ c. soy sauce
¼ c. or more red wine
  vinegar
2 Tbsp. vegetable oil
2 Tbsp. Worcestershire
  sauce
1 large clove garlic, sliced
Pepper to taste
Chopped green onion or
  chives (optional)
Chopped dill weed
  (optional)
Celery seed (optional)
1 (1½ lb.) flank steak,
  trimmed

Mix all ingredients, except the steak, in the pan in which meat is to be marinated. Marinate flank steak, turning occasionally for 2 to 12 hours in the refrigerator. Broil meat over hot coals for 5 minutes per side for rare meat. Slice meat on the diagonal across the grain and serve. Serves 3 to 4.

CHARCOAL GRILLED TENDERLOIN

3 to 4 lb. whole beef
  tenderloin
2 cloves garlic, minced
Cooking oil

Rub tenderloin with oil and garlic. Cook on prepared charcoal grill until desired doneness. Turn 2 to 3 times during cooking. Will take 30 to 45 minutes. Do not cook on a too hot grill. Slice and serve immediately. Serve with Bernaise sauce, if desired. Serves 8.

BARBECUED LONDON BROIL

⅓ c. white vinegar
⅓ c. vegetable oil
3 Tbsp. packed brown
  sugar
3 Tbsp. soy sauce
2 medium onions, sliced
1 clove garlic, crushed
½ tsp. coarsely ground
  pepper
1½-lb. beef flank steak

Mix all ingredients except beef flank steak; pour over beef. Cover and refrigerate, turning beef 2 or 3 times, at least 4 hours.

Remove beef and onions; reserve marinade. Cover and grill beef 4 to 5 inches from medium coals, turning and brushing 2 or 3 times with reserved marinade, until desired doneness, 10 to 15 minutes for medium. Cook and stir onions in grill pan on grill until warm. Cut beef diagonally across the grain into very thin slices; top with onions.

14 BEEF

SESAME-MARINATED BEEF ROAST

⅓ c. (2¼-oz. pkg.)
  sesame seed
½ c. salad oil
½ c. soy sauce
⅓ c. lemon juice
2 Tbsp. white wine
  vinegar
1 Tbsp. sugar
2 cloves garlic, mashed
1 medium-sized onion,
  sliced
4 lb. sirloin tip roast

For the marinade, heat sesame seed in salad oil just long enough to brown the seeds slightly. Combine with soy sauce, lemon juice, vinegar, sugar, garlic, and onion. Pour over meat; cover, and marinate in refrigerator about 24 hours, turning meat occasionally.
To barbecue, drain roast, saving the marinade. Arrange glowing coals in a ring around the perimeter of the fire grate in your grill and place a foil drip pan in the center. Insert meat thermometer into center of roast and place on grill over drip pan. Cover barbecue and regulate dampers to maintain a temperature of 350 degrees to 375 degrees. You may need a few additional burning briquettes during last part of cooking. It will take about 1½ hours for meat to reach 130 degrees (rare). Baste occasionally with marinade. Serves 6.

BEEF SHORT RIBS

1½ to 2 lb. beef short ribs
1 small can V-8 juice
2 onions, cut into fourths
4 carrots, cut into 2-inch
  slices
2 stalks celery, cut into 2-
  inch slices
2 potatoes, cut into 6
  pieces
Salt
Pepper
¼ c. barbecue sauce

Brown short ribs in broiler pan under broiler, turning to brown all sides. Season well with salt and pepper; place in roaster pan, covering the short ribs with roaster lid. Bake in oven at 350 degrees. After baking 1 hour, add onions, carrots, celery, potatoes, and V-8 juice. Can also add ¼ cup barbecue sauce. Cook about 3 to 4 hours.

BARBECUED SHORT RIBS

3 lb. short ribs
1 c. water
½ c. vinegar
1 Tbsp. prepared
  horseradish
1 tsp. salt
2 Tbsp. parsley, chopped
1 c. tomato sauce
1 Tbsp. sugar
1 Tbsp. mustard
¼ tsp. pepper
2 onions, finely chopped

Wipe short ribs with damp cloth and place in deep bowl. Combine tomato sauce, water, vinegar, sugar, horseradish, mustard, seasonings, onions, and parsley. Pour over ribs. Let stand in refrigerator at least 4 hours or overnight. Place in shallow baking pan. Cover and cook until tender, about 3 hours. Add more water as needed. To serve, place in serving dish. Skim excess fat off sauce, then spoon sauce over ribs.

MARINATED SHORT RIBS

5 lb. beef short ribs
1½ c. red wine vinegar
2 Tbsp. browning sauce
2 tsp. salt
½ tsp. dried basil
2 Tbsp. prepared mustard
2 cloves garlic, crushed
2 bay leaves

Place ribs in a shallow container. Mix remaining ingredients. Pour over ribs. Cover. Refrigerate 2 hours. Grill over moderate heat for 1 hour, turning and brushing with marinade occasionally. Serves 4 to 6.

SHISH KABOBS

2 to 2½ lb. beef, cut in
   2-inch cubes, marinated
Green peppers cut in
   1-inch squares
Cherry tomatoes
Large fresh mushrooms
Whole tiny onions, peeled
Bacon squares

Arrange marinated meat on skewers, alternating vegetables and bacon squares. Have skewers 3 to 4 inches above fire. Broil 15 to 20 minutes, turning frequently to cook meat evenly. Brush occasionally with marinade.

SHISH KABOB MEAT MARINADE

1½ c. salad oil
¾ c. soy sauce
¼ c. Worcestershire sauce
2 Tbsp. dry mustard
2½ tsp. salt
1 Tbsp. freshly ground
   pepper
1½ tsp. parsley flakes
½ c. wine vinegar
1 clove garlic, crushed
⅓ c. fresh lemon juice

Combine all ingredients and heat. Cool. Pour over meat and marinate 4 hours or overnight. Yields 3½ cups.

BEEF AND CORN KABOBS

½ c. vegetable oil
¼ c. red wine vinegar
1 Tbsp. chopped fresh or
1 tsp. dried thyme
leaves
½ tsp. ground red pepper
(cayenne)
1 clove garlic, finely
chopped
1½ lb. beef boneless top
round steak, cut into 1-
inch cubes
4 small ears corn, husks
removed
2 bell peppers, cut into
1½-inch pieces

Mix oil, vinegar, thyme, red pepper and garlic in medium glass or plastic bowl. Add beef; stir to coat with marinade. Cover and refrigerate at least 4 hours, stirring occasionally.

Cut each ear of corn into 3 pieces. Remove beef from marinade; reserve marinade. Thread beef alternately with corn and bell peppers about ¼ inch apart on six 11-inch metal skewers. Brush generously with marinade.

Cover and grill 4 to 5 inches from medium coals 15 to 20 minutes for medium doneness, turning the kabobs frequently and brushing with marinade. Serves 6.

BARBECUED BEEF

5 lb. beef brisket
2 Tbsp. Liquid Smoke
½ to 1 tsp. seasoned salt
½ tsp. celery powder
½ tsp. garlic powder
1 small onion, chopped
2 Tbsp. Worcestershire
sauce
1½ Tbsp. brown sugar
½ tsp. dry mustard
1 c. ketchup
1 c. beef broth
1 tsp. celery seed
3 Tbsp. butter

Rub brisket with liquid smoke. Sprinkle with seasoned salt, celery powder, garlic powder and chopped onion. Wrap tightly in foil and place in glass baking dish. Refrigerate overnight. Bake wrapped brisket at 250 degrees for 5 hours. Combine remaining ingredients in a saucepan over medium heat and simmer 10 minutes to make a sauce. Open foil, coat brisket with sauce and bake uncovered at 325 degrees for 1 hour. Cool and slice to serve. May also be sliced very thin and served on hard rolls. Serves 10 to 12.

BARBECUE FOR A CROWD

5 lb. rump roast
5 lb. pork roast

Barbecue Sauce:
1/2 c. margarine, melted
4 med. onions, chopped
8 cloves garlic
1 c. Worcestershire sauce
1 c. vinegar
4 dashes red pepper
4 tsp. salt
8 c. boiling water
4 c. ketchup
4 tsp. dry mustard
8 tsp. chili powder

Cook roasts for about 6 hours at 325 degrees until done. May need to cover beef roast with aluminum foil to keep outside from becoming crisp. Drain fat from roasts and shred meat.

Barbecue Sauce: In a large kettle, saute onion and garlic in margarine until translucent. Add remaining ingredients. Bring to a boil. Add shredded meat. Reduce heat and cook to desired consistency. Serve on buns or rice. Makes approximately 35 servings on buns, or 16 to 18 on rice. Can freeze.

POT ROAST BARBECUE

4 to 8 lb. pot roast,
   venison, beef, pork, or
   turkey breast
1 qt. water or beer
1 Tbsp. garlic powder
1 Tbsp. mustard seeds
1 Tbsp. red pepper
1 Tbsp. dill seed
1 c. white vinegar
2 c. onion, chopped
2 c. celery, chopped
2 c. ketchup
1/2 c. Worcestershire
   sauce
1/2 c. brown sugar

Trim excess fat from meat. In a separate pot make barbecue sauce. Place meat in a large covered roasting pan. Preheat oven to 300 degrees. Cover meat with sauce. Place lid on pan and place in oven. Bake for 2 to 3 hours until meat is done. Freezes well for future meals.

BARBECUED ROAST

4 to 5 lb. roast
1 bottle barbecue sauce
Garlic powder
Red pepper
Minced onions
Jalapeno pepper
Parsley flakes
Salt
Black pepper
Foil

Line a bowl with foil. Add roast and all seasonings. Pour barbecue sauce over roast. Cover with foil and marinate for 4 to 5 hours or until meat is tender. Bake at 325° for 5 to 6 hours. Serve leftovers on buns.

TEXAS BRISKET WITH BARBECUE SAUCE

1½ tsp. salt
1½ tsp. pepper
2 Tbsp. chili powder
1 tsp. bay leaves, crushed
2 Tbsp. Liquid Smoke
4 lb. beef brisket

Barbecue Sauce:
3 Tbsp. brown sugar
1 (14-oz.) bottle catsup
½ c. water
2 Tbsp. Liquid Smoke
Salt and pepper to taste
4 Tbsp. Worcestershire
   sauce
3 tsp. dry mustard
2 tsp. celery seed
6 Tbsp. butter
¼ tsp. cayenne pepper

Combine salt, pepper, chili powder, and bay leaves. Rub meat completely with Liquid Smoke. Place meat, fat side up, in a large roasting pan. Sprinkle dry seasoning mixture on top. Cover tightly. Bake for 4 hours at 325 degrees. Scrape seasoning off meat and cut in very thin slices across the grain. Serve with barbecue sauce.

Combine all ingredients. Bring to a boil, stirring occasionally. Cook for 10 minutes. Serve with sliced brisket. This is good by itself or on onion rolls. Serves 6.

BARBECUED BRISKET

6 lb. brisket
3 Tbsp. liquid smoke
2 Tbsp. Worcestershire
1 tsp. garlic powder
1 tsp. onion salt
2 tsp. celery salt
2 tsp. freshly ground
   pepper

Barbecue Sauce:
1 c. catsup
1 tsp. salt
1 tsp. celery seed
¼ c. brown sugar
¼ c. Worcestershire sauce
2 c. water
1 onion, chopped
¼ c. vinegar

Sprinkle brisket with the liquid smoke, Worcestershire sauce, garlic powder, onion salt, celery salt, and pepper. Cover with foil and refrigerate overnight. Bake, covered, for 5 hours at 275 degrees. Drain off grease. Uncover and bake 1 hour with barbecue sauce.

Barbecue Sauce: In a medium cooking pot, combine all sauce ingredients. Bring to a boil; boil for 15 minutes, stirring constantly. Spread sauce over brisket.

BARBECUED BEEF BRISKET

1 c. ketchup
1 c. chili sauce
1 c. water
1/2 c. lemon juice
1/4 c. brown sugar, packed
1 Tbsp. Worcestershire
   sauce
1 Tbsp. Dijon mustard
1 (1.4 oz.) pkg. onion
   soup mix
1 (5 to 6 lb.) brisket

Mix first 8 ingredients and simmer 10 minutes or longer. Trim most of fat off meat, leaving a thin layer. Put meat on grill about 8 inches from coals. Cook 4 to 5 hours or until meat is tender. Turn meat every 20 minutes and baste with sauce each time you turn it. Regular mustard may be used instead of Dijon. Sauce is good on ribs or chicken.

BARBECUED MEATBALLS

1 lb. ground beef
1 slice of bread crumbs in
   1/4 c. milk
1 onion, chopped
1/2 green pepper, chopped
Pinch of salt and pepper

Sauce:
1/2 c. catsup
1/4 c. vinegar
1/2 c. water
2 Tbsp. Worcestershire
   sauce
Hot pepper

In a medium bowl, mix together the beef, bread crumbs, onion, green pepper, and salt and pepper. Form into 1-inch meatballs, and place in an oven proof dish. Cover meatballs with sauce; place cover on dish. Cook in a 375 degree oven for 45 minutes.

Sauce: In a small bow, mix thoroughly together the sauce ingredients.

BARBECUED SLOPPY JOES

1 lb. ground round
1/2 c. onion, chopped
1/4 c. celery, chopped
1/4 c. green pepper,
   chopped
1 (8 oz.) can tomato
   sauce
1/4 c. catsup
1 Tbsp. vinegar
1 Tbsp. sugar
1 1/2 tsp. Worcestershire
   sauce
1 tsp. salt
1/4 tsp. pepper

Brown meat; add vegetables. Cook until vegetables are tender. Add seasonings and remaining ingredients. Simmer for 30 minutes.

BARBECUE FOR SANDWICHES

1½ lb. hamburger
¾ c. rolled oats
1 c. milk
3 Tbsp. onion, chopped
1½ tsp. salt
½ tsp. pepper

Barbecue Sauce:
1 Tbsp. Worcestershire
  sauce
3 Tbsp. vinegar
2 Tbsp. sugar
1 c. catsup
½ c. water
6 tsp. onion, chopped

Combine the hamburger, oats, milk, onion, salt, and pepper. Place in skillet, and cook until meat is thoroughly browned. Stir barbecue sauce into cooked meat mixture, and simmer for 15 minutes.

Sauce: Combine all ingredients.

BARBECUED SANDWICHES

1 med. onion, chopped
2 Tbsp. butter
2 Tbsp. vinegar
2 Tbsp. brown sugar
4 Tbsp. lemon juice
1 small bottle catsup
3 Tbsp. Worcestershire
  sauce
½ Tbsp. mustard
1 c. water
1 c. celery, chopped
Salt and red pepper to
  taste

Brown chopped onion in melted butter. Add the remaining ingredients and let simmer until celery is tender. Add about 3 cups (more or less as desired) chopped well done roast beef or pork roast. Serve hot on hamburger buns.

BARBECUED MEAT LOAF

1½ lb. ground chuck
1 c. fresh bread crumbs
1 med. onion, chopped
Salt and pepper
½ (8 oz.) can tomato
  sauce (4 oz.)
1 egg, beaten

Barbecue Sauce:
½ (8 oz.) can tomato
  sauce (4 oz.)
1 can water
2 Tbsp. mustard
2 Tbsp. brown sugar
2 Tbsp. vinegar

Barbecue Sauce: In a small mixing bowl, thoroughly mix together all sauce ingredients.

Meat Loaf: Mix the ground chuck, bread crumbs, onion, salt and pepper, ½ can tomato sauce, and egg together and shape into loaf. Pour the barbecue sauce over the loaf.

POULTRY

SOUTH-OF-THE-BORDER GRILLED CHICKEN SALAD

¼ c. soy sauce
¼ c. water
2 Tbsp. lime juice (1 lime)
½ tsp. freshly ground
    pepper
⅛ tsp. garlic powder
4 large skinless, boneless
    chicken breast halves
    (about 1 lb.)
2 c. mesquite chips or
    other wood chips for
    barbecuing
½ tsp. freshly ground
    pepper
8 c. torn mixed salad
    greens
¾ c. mild salsa
¼ c. buttermilk salad
    dressing
1 red or green sweet
    pepper, sliced into thin
    rings
2 green onions, thinly
    sliced

In a large, shallow container, mix together soy sauce, water, lime juice, ½ tsp. pepper and garlic powder. Rinse chicken and pat dry. Add to marinade, turning once. Cover; marinate in refrigerator for 6 to 24 hours.

Soak chips in water for 1 hour. Drain. Add .chips to medium coals. Grill chicken directly over medium coals for 12 to 15 minutes or till done, turning once. Chill chicken. Slice chicken diagonally into bite-size strips. Season with pepper.

To assemble salad, on a large platter, layer in order: greens, salsa, salad dressing, pepper rings, chicken, and onion. Serves 4.

CRISPY GRILLED CHICKEN

Orange-Ginger Marinade:
¼ c. orange marmalade
¼ c. orange juice
2 Tbsp. soy sauce
1 tsp. ground ginger
1½ tsp. Dijon-style
    mustard
1 clove garlic, minced

Chicken:
Chicken thighs and
    drumsticks, skinned
    (about 3½ lb.)
1 c. corn flakes, lightly
    crushed

Combine all ingredients in a small bowl. Place chicken in zip-top plastic bag. Pour marinade over chicken; close bag securely, turning to coat well. Refrigerate 2 hours. Remove chicken from marinade and roll in corn flakes. Pat extra corn flakes on if necessary to make a solid coating. Place chicken in lightly oiled disposable aluminum foil pan; cover loosely with foil. Cook on covered grill over medium, direct heat 30 to 40 minutes or until cooked through. Uncover last 10 minutes. Serve hot or cold.

GRILLED MARINATED CHICKEN

14 to 16 chicken pieces

Marinade:
½ c. vegetable oil
½ c. lemon juice
½ c. wine vinegar
¼ c. soy sauce
1 tsp. salt
½ tsp. pepper
1 tsp. basil
1 tsp. marjoram
1 tsp. savory
1 tsp. thyme

In a shallow baking dish large enough to hold the chicken pieces in a single layer, mix ingredients for Marinade. Place chicken in dish and marinate for 4 hours, turning occasionally. Drain Marinade and reserve. Bake chicken in same dish for 30 minutes at 325°. Place chicken on grill and baste often with Marinade. Cook for 30 minutes, turning occasionally.

Serves 6 to 8.

BARBECUED CHICKEN

1 fryer (3 to 3½ lb.)
¼ c. shortening
1 c. onion, chopped
½ c. celery, chopped
1 c. water
1 c. catsup
¼ c. lemon juice
2 Tbsp. brown sugar
3 Tbsp. Worcestershire
　sauce
2 Tbsp. vinegar
1 tsp. salt
1½ tsp. prepared mustard
Dash red pepper

Brown chicken in hot fat; set aside. Combine remaining ingredients; simmer 30 minutes. Place chicken in shallow baking dish. Pour sauce over. Bake uncovered at 350 degrees for 1 hour or until tender. Serves 6.

BARBECUED CHICKEN

2 fryers (3 to 3½ lb. each)
Flour
Pepper
2 c. water
¼ c. vinegar
2 Tbsp. Worcestershire
　sauce
1 med. onion, sliced
Juice of 1 lemon
Red pepper
Salt
¼ lb. butter

Dress as for broiling 2 frying chickens. Dust with flour and pepper. Place in broiling pan with water, vinegar, Worcestershire sauce, onion, lemon juice, red pepper, salt, and butter.

Bake at 450 degrees for 20 minutes. Reduce heat to 300 degrees and cook for 2 hours, basting with sauce frequently. Serve on platter with sauce poured over chicken; garnish with parsley and sliced tomatoes.

OVEN BARBECUED CHICKEN

½ tsp. dry mustard
½ tsp. chili powder
½ tsp. salt
½ tsp. celery salt
½ tsp. cayenne pepper
½ c. butter
1 Tbsp. horseradish
2 Tbsp. Worcestershire
   sauce
4 Tbsp. tomato catsup

Mix all ingredients and set aside to cool. Cut chicken in half. Sear on both sides in hot fat, turning and basting often with sauce mixture, until chicken is brown and tender. After removing chicken, add 1 cup water for gravy.

GRILLED LEMON CHICKEN

1 c. oil
½ c. lemon juice
1 Tbsp. salt
1 tsp. paprika
2 tsp. basil
2 tsp. onion powder
½ tsp. thyme
1 clove garlic
1 lemon, sliced
3 chickens, cut for grill

Blend marinade ingredients. Pour over chicken and sliced lemon. Marinate overnight in refrigerator. Grill as usual, basting with marinade.

GRILLED CHICKEN BREASTS

2 tsp. Dijon mustard
¼ tsp. ground pepper
6 boneless chicken
   breasts
⅓ c. margarine
1 tsp. dried whole
   tarragon
2 tsp. lemon juice
½ tsp. garlic salt

Spread mustard and pepper over chicken breast. Cover and refrigerate 2 to 4 hours. Melt margarine over medium heat. Stir in tarragon, lemon juice and garlic salt. Cook, uncovered, over low heat for 5 minutes, stirring occasionally. Remove from heat. Baste chicken with sauce. Grill over medium coals 50 to 55 minutes, or until done. Turn and baste every 10 minutes with remaining sauce.

GRILLED LEMON-LIME CHICKEN

1 (3½ lb.) chicken,
  quartered
1 lemon
1 lime
3 Tbsp. extra-virgin olive
  oil
1 garlic clove, crushed
1 tsp. salt
½ tsp. freshly ground
  pepper
⅛ tsp. cayenne

Rinse chicken and pat dry. Grate colored zest from lemon and lime into a medium bowl. Add juice from lemon and lime, olive oil, garlic, salt, pepper, and cayenne. Mix well. Add chicken and turn to coat. Cover and marinate, turning occasionally, 1 to 2 hours at room temperature, or up to 12 hours refrigerated.

Prepare a hot fire. Remove chicken from marinade and place on an oiled grill set 4 to 6 inches from coals. Grill, turning and basting with marinade every 10 minutes, until chicken is browned outside and white throughout with no trace of pink near bone, 40 to 45 minutes. Serves 4.

HONEY-GLAZED CHICKEN

½ c. honey
2 Tbsp. vegetable oil
2 Tbsp. prepared mustard
2 Tbsp. lemon juice
½ tsp. grated lemon peel
½ tsp. salt
2½-lb. broiler-fryer
  chicken, cut-up

Mix all ingredients except chicken pieces. Cover and grill chicken, bone sides down, 5 to 6 inches from medium coals, 15 to 30 minutes; turn chicken. Cover and grill, turning and brushing 2 or 3 times with honey mixture, until chicken is done, 20 to 40 minutes longer. Serves 6.

CHICKEN BREASTS PAPRIKA

¼ c. margarine or butter,
  softened
1 Tbsp. paprika
1 tsp. salt
¼ tsp. pepper
2 cloves garlic, crushed
3 whole chicken breasts
  (about 2 lb.), cut into
  halves

Mix all ingredients except chicken breasts. Cover and grill chicken, bone sides down, 5 to 6 inches from medium coals, 10 to 20 minutes; turn chicken. Cover and grill, turning and brushing 2 or 3 times with margarine mixture, until chicken is done, 25 to 35 minutes. Serves 6.

GRILLED LIGHT CHICKEN

⅓ c. fresh lemon juice
¼ c. olive oil
2 cloves garlic, minced
1½ Tbsp. rosemary, finely
  chopped
1½ Tbsp. tarragon, finely
  chopped
½ tsp. black pepper,
  freshly ground
1 (3½ lb.) fryer, split in
  half, skinned
1 (12 oz.) bottle barbecue
  sauce

In container, combine lemon juice, olive oil, garlic, rosemary, tarragon, and pepper. Cover container tightly; shake vigorously. Pour marinade over top of chicken; turn to coat both sides. Cover and refrigerate 4 hours or overnight.

Position wire rack 4 inches to 6 inches from heat. Preheat grill. Place marinated chicken on rack. Grill 30-45 minutes, turning frequently. Brush lightly with sauce 20 minutes before serving. Serves 4.

TERIYAKI CHICKEN

1 (8-oz.) can crushed
  pineapple, undrained
¼ c. teriyaki sauce
2 Tbsp. lemon juice
2 Tbsp. red wine vinegar
2 cloves garlic, minced
1 Tbsp. olive oil
¼ tsp. mesquite liquid
  smoke
6 chicken breast halves,
  skinned and boned

Combine first 7 ingredients; place in a shallow container or a heavy-duty zip-top plastic bag. Add chicken; cover or seal, and chill 1 to 2 hours, turning occasionally. Remove chicken from marinade. grill, covered, over medium coals (300 degrees to 400 degrees) for 4 to 5 minutes on each side. Yield: 6 servings.

SPICY CHICKEN BREASTS

4 chicken breast halves,
  bones in, skin on
Salt and pepper
¼ c. fresh orange juice
2 Tbsp. parsley, chopped
2 Tbsp. olive oil
2 to 3 small fresh hot
  chili peppers, preferably
  a combination of red
  and green, seeded and
  minced

Rinse chicken with cold water and pat dry. Place in a glass baking dish and season with salt and pepper. In a small bowl, combine orange juice with parsley, olive oil, and chilies. Cover with plastic wrap and marinate 2 to 4 hours at room temperature, or overnight in refrigerator.

Prepare grill. Remove chicken from marinade, brushing off most of chilies and parsley clinging to meat. Reserve marinade and chilies for basting.

Set chicken skin side down on an oiled grill over hot coals and cook until nicely browned on bottom, about 6 to 8 minutes. Turn over and begin brushing with reserved marinade. Continue cooking and basting until chicken is just cooked through, about 10 minutes longer.

GRILLED CHICKEN FAJITAS

4 (1 lb.) skinless boneless
   chicken breast halves,
   cut into 4 x ¼-inch
   strips
1 med. onion, cut into
   ¼-inch slices
¼ c. lime juice
1 Tbsp. vegetable oil
1 tsp. chili powder
8 (8-inch) flour tortillas
1 c. salsa
½ c. guacamole
   (optional)
3 tomatoes, finely diced
Grated cheddar cheese

Place chicken and onion in shallow glass or plastic dish. Mix lime juice, oil, and chili powder. Pour over chicken and onion. Cover and refrigerate 1 hour.

Remove chicken and onion from marinade; reserve marinade. Grill chicken and onion 4 to 6 inches from medium coals 8 to 10 minutes, brushing frequently with marinade, until chicken is done. Place chicken and onion on tortillas. Add tomatoes and cheese, as desired; fold. Top with salsa and guacamole. Serves 4.

HONEY-BARBECUED WINGS

3 lb. chicken wings
⅓ c. honey
1 tsp. dry mustard
1 tsp. paprika
1 tsp. chili powder
1 tsp. salt
½ tsp. pepper
¼ c. water
3 Tbsp. ketchup
2 Tbsp. butter
3 Tbsp. lemon juice or
   vinegar
2 Tbsp. Worcestershire
   sauce
2 garlic cloves, finely
   minced

Preheat oven to 325 degrees. Prepare wings by removing tips and cutting wings in halves.

Combine sauce ingredients in medium saucepan. Bring to boil and remove from heat. Dip wings in sauce, then lay them in a roasting pan. Cover with remaining sauce. Bake for 45 minutes, basting often. Turn wings over and bake another 15 to 20 minutes or until wings are well-browned. Serves 4.

APRICOT-GLAZED CORNISH HENS

4 large apricots (1 lb.)
1 garlic clove
1 (1" by ½") piece peeled
 ginger root or ½ tsp.
 ground ginger
¼ c. apricot preserves
2 Tbsp. soy sauce
4 (1½-lb.) fresh or frozen
 (thawed) Rock Cornish
 hens

About 1½ hours before serving, prepare outdoor grill for barbecuing. Remove pits from apricots. In blender at high speed or in food processor with knife blade attached, blend apricots, garlic, ginger root, apricot preserves, and soy sauce until smooth.

Remove giblets and necks from hens; refrigerate to use another day. With kitchen shears, cut each hen in half. Rinse hens with running cold water; pat dry with paper towels.

Place hens on grill over medium heat; cook 35 minutes, turning hens often. Brush hens frequently with apricot mixture during last 10 minutes of grilling.

YOGURT-GLAZED TURKEY BREAST

1 turkey breast half,
 about 2 lb. (with back
 and rib portions)
½ tsp. salt
⅛ tsp. freshly ground
 pepper
1 garlic clove, minced
¼ c. plain yogurt
1 tsp. Dijon mustard
½ c. orange juice
1 Tbsp. fresh sage leaves,
 chopped, or 1 tsp. dried
1 tsp. honey

Rinse turkey breast with cold water and pat dry. Season with salt and pepper and place in a baking dish. In a small bowl, combine garlic, yogurt, mustard, orange juice, sage, and honey. Brush marinade over turkey, cover with plastic wrap, and refrigerate 24 to 48 hours.

Prepare a hot fire. Remove turkey from marinade, reserving marinade. Grill turkey over indirect heat, turning at least once, until browned outside and just cooked through inside, about 40 to 50 minutes total. Baste with reserved marinade during last 10 minutes of cooking. Serves 3 to 4.

GRILLED TURKEY TENDERLOINS WITH PINEAPPLE SALSA

6 turkey breast
 tenderloins, cut about 1
 inch thick
1½ tsp. salt
⅛ tsp. freshly ground
 pepper
½ c. olive oil
¼ c. fresh lemon juice
½ c. onion, coarsely
 chopped
Grilled Pineapple Salsa

Rinse turkey with cold water and pat dry. Season with salt and pepper. Combine olive oil, lemon juice, and onion in a shallow pan. Add turkey and turn to coat. Cover and marinate at room temperature for 1 hour.

Prepare a hot fire. Grill turkey over hot coals, turning once, until browned outside and just cooked through, about 5 minutes per side. Top each portion with a spoonful of Grilled Pineapple Salsa before serving.

28   POULTRY

GRILLED PINEAPPLE SALSA

1 medium pineapple, skin
  removed
1 medium red onion,
  finely chopped
2 jalapeno peppers,
  seeded and minced
1 garlic clove, minced
½ c. fresh cilantro or
  mint, chopped
1 tsp. sugar
¼ tsp. salt

Prepare a hot fire. Slice pineapple into rounds ½ to ¾ inch thick. When coals are covered with gray ash, place pineapple slices on an oiled rack set 4 to 6 inches from coals. Grill, turning once or twice, until lightly browned on both sides, about 10 minutes. Let cool, then finely dice grilled pineapple, discarding tough center core.

Combine pineapple, red onion, jalapeno peppers, garlic, cilantro, sugar, and salt in a medium bowl. Marinate at least 2 hours at room temperature, or cover and refrigerate up to 3 days.

RED HOT BARBECUED TURKEY WINGS

4 to 5 lb. turkey wings
½ c. Tabasco
1 lb. butter
Salt and pepper
Cayenne pepper

Preheat oven to 400 degrees. Salt and pepper each turkey wing. Melt butter. Add Tabasco and cayenne pepper; drizzle over wings in a baking pan. Bake for 1½ to 2 hours. Reduce oven temperature to 350 degrees after 45 minutes.

GRILLED TURKEY BREAST

1 (5 to 7 lb.) turkey breast
3 c. soy sauce
2 c. Worcestershire sauce
1 c. lemon juice

For best results, use fresh turkey breast. Debone both halves of turkey breast, leaving skin on. Combine the last three ingredients for marinade sauce. Marinade both breast halves in sealed baggie or sealed dish for approximately 3 hours. Place breasts on hot grill, skin side up. Turn every 25 minutes, brushing with the marinade on every turn. Cook 2 hours. Remove skin and slice.

GRILLED TURKEY BURGERS

1 lb. ground turkey
¼ c. dry bread crumbs
2 tsp. instant minced
  onion
1 tsp. prepared
  horseradish
½ tsp. ground sage

Mix all ingredients. Shape mixture into 4 patties, each about 4 inches in diameter. Grill patties about 4 inches from medium coals, turning once, until desired doneness, 5 to 7 minutes on each side for medium. Serve in hamburger buns with cranberry relish, if desired.

PORK AND HAM

PINEAPPLE BARBECUED SPARERIBS

10 lb. spareribs
Water
12 whole black peppers
6 whole cloves
2 bay leaves
2 cloves garlic

Place spareribs in water, almost covering the spareribs. Season with peppers, cloves, bay leaves, and garlic. Bring to a boil; cover, and simmer for 30 minutes, or until almost tender. Drain, then cover and refrigerate.

Arrange spareribs on the grill over hot coals; cook about 30 minutes, turning occasionally. During the last 15 minutes, baste with Pineapple Barbecue Sauce (recipe follows). Cook until ribs are glazed and tender. Remove onto warm platter. Serves 10 to 12.

PINEAPPLE BARBECUE SAUCE

2 Tbsp. brown sugar
2 medium onions, finely
  chopped
2/3 c. soy sauce
1/4 c. catsup
1 (1 lb.) can crushed
  pineapple (including
  syrup)
2/3 c. wine vinegar
1/2 tsp. black pepper
1 tsp. salt

Combine above ingredients. Makes about 4 cups.

SPARERIBS ON THE GRILL

Pork spareribs (about 3/4
  to 1 lb. for each serving
  desired)
Barbecue Sauce (recipe
  follows)*

Cut ribs into sections. Wrap uncooked ribs securely in aluminum foil. Grill 30 minutes, turning once. Unwrap; place ribs on grill. Cook about 20 to 30 minutes or until browned on all sides, turning frequently and basting with barbecue sauce often.

BARBECUE SAUCE FOR SPARERIBS

½ c. catsup
½ c. water
¼ c. vinegar
3 Tbsp. sugar
½ c. onion, chopped
1½ tsp. Worcestershire
  sauce
½ c. green pepper

Mix all ingredients and pour over meat.

CHERRY-GLAZED SPARERIBS

6 lb. pork spareribs
1 lb. dark sweet cherries
¼ c. red wine vinegar
¼ c. light molasses
¼ c. chili sauce
3 Tbsp. soy sauce
⅛ tsp. hot pepper sauce
2 green onions, chopped
Green onions for garnish

Early in day or day ahead, cut pork spareribs into 2-rib portions. In 8-quart saucepan or Dutch oven, cover spareribs with water; over high heat, heat to boiling. Reduce heat to low; cover and simmer 1 hour or until spareribs are fork-tender. Remove ribs to platter; cover and refrigerate.

About 1 hour before serving, prepare outdoor grill for barbecuing. Reserve several cherries with stems for garnish. Stem and pit remaining cherries. In blender at medium speed or in food processor with knife blade attached, blend cherries until smooth; pour into bowl. Stir in red wine vinegar, molasses, chili sauce, hot pepper sauce, soy sauce, and chopped green onions. Place spareribs on grill over medium heat; cook 20 minutes or until heated through, turning ribs often and brushing with cherry sauce frequently during the last 10 minutes of cooking. Garnish with green onions and reserved cherries. Yield: 6 servings.

KANSAS CITY-STYLE SPARERIBS

6 garlic cloves, crushed
8 to 9 lb. pork spareribs
   (about 3 racks)
2 tsp. salt
½ tsp. pepper, freshly
   ground
1 c. (packed) dark brown
   sugar
¾ c. coarse grainy
   mustard
⅓ c. cider vinegar
¼ c. molasses
1½ Tbsp. dry mustard

Preheat oven to 350°. Rub garlic into both sides of ribs and season with salt and pepper. Arrange ribs meaty side down on a large baking sheet. Bake 1 hour, turning ribs after 20 minutes. (Ribs can be baked a day ahead. Remove to a rack and let drain and cool. Then wrap in plastic wrap and refrigerate.)

In a medium saucepan, combine brown sugar, grainy mustard, vinegar, molasses, and dry mustard. Bring to a boil, reduce heat, and simmer, stirring to dissolve sugar, 5 minutes. Remove glaze from heat and let cool slightly.

Prepare a hot fire. Place prebaked ribs meaty side up on an oiled grill set 4 to 6 inches from coals. Spread one third of glaze over ribs and cook until bottom is browned, about 5 minutes. Turn, spread half of remaining glaze over ribs, and cook until meaty side is browned and crisp, about 5 minutes. Turn again and spread remaining glaze on top. Grill until bottom side is well browned and crisp, about 5 minutes longer. Cut into individual ribs or portions for serving.

COUNTRY STYLE SPARERIBS WITH SAUCE

4 lb. country style ribs
1 Tbsp. butter
1 clove garlic
2 Tbsp. chopped onion
¾ c. catsup
1 tsp. chili powder
2 Tbsp. brown sugar
2 Tbsp. Worcestershire
   sauce
1 Tbsp. prepared mustard
1 tsp. celery seed
¼ tsp. salt
Dash of bottled hot
   pepper sauce
1 Tbsp. ReaLemon lemon
   juice

Simmer ribs about one hour in covered pot of salted water. May do this ahead and chill. In saucepan, melt butter, add garlic and onion. Add remaining ingredients and bring to a boil; set aside. Drain ribs. Grill over medium coals about 10 minutes on each side, brushing often with sauce till well coated. If ribs were chilled before cooking, grill 15 to 18 minutes on each side. May substitute any meat for the ribs, chicken, steak, etc.

Serves 6 to 8.

BARBECUED CHIPPED HAM SANDWICHES

1½ lb. chipped ham
3 Tbsp. oil
¼ c. onion, chopped

Sauce:
1 Tbsp. sugar
1 tsp. dry mustard
1 tsp. paprika
½ c. ketchup
½ c. water
1 Tbsp. Worcestershire
　　sauce
Salt and pepper

Saute onion in oil; add ham. Combine sugar, mustard, paprika, ketchup, water, Worcestershire sauce, salt, and pepper. Cook sauce for 5 minutes. Add meat. Simmer together 15 minutes. Serve on buns. Top with a slice of cheese if desired.

BARBECUED SPARERIBS

2 garlic cloves, minced
2 Tbsp. butter, melted
2 Tbsp. prepared mustard
¼ c. (packed) brown
　　sugar
1 c. ketchup
¾ c. chili sauce
1 Tbsp. celery seeds
2 Tbsp. Worcestershire
　　sauce
2 dashes of hot pepper
　　sauce
1 tsp. salt
1½ c. water
4 lb. spareribs or loin
　　back ribs

In a medium saucepan, saute garlic in butter over medium heat until softened but not browned, 2 to 3 minutes. Add mustard, brown sugar, ketchup, chili sauce, celery seeds, Worcestershire, hot sauce, salt, and water, and bring to a boil. If made in advance, let cool, cover, and refrigerate until ready to baste ribs.

Prepare a medium fire. Place ribs, bone side down, on an oiled grill set 6 inches from coals. Grill until brown, about 20 minutes; turn meaty side down and cook until browned, about 15 minutes longer. Turn meaty side up again and continue to grill without turning 20 to 30 minutes, basting with sauce very 5 to 10 minutes. Brush sauce on both sides of ribs and let cook 2 to 3 minutes on each side to glaze well.

TEXAS PORK STEAKS

1 tsp. chili powder
½ tsp. garlic powder
½ tsp. dry mustard
½ tsp. salt
¼ tsp. pepper
2 lb. pork blade or arm
　　steaks, ½ inch thick

Mix all ingredients except pork steaks; rub this mixture on pork. Cover and grill pork 5 to 6 inches from medium coals, turning 3 or 4 times, until pork is done and no longer pink in center (170°), 25 to 35 minutes. Serves 6.

GRILLED PORK ROAST

2-4 lb. boneless pork rib-
  end roast

Basting Sauce:
¾ c. chili sauce
¼ c. cider vinegar
1 tsp. dry mustard

Prepare medium hot coals in covered grill, banking coals on sides of grill. Place drip pan in center of grill bed.

Mix together basting sauce ingredients. Place pork on grill over drip pan. Close grill; roast pork for 45 minutes - 1½ hours, basting every 10-15 minutes with basting sauce. Remove pork from grill when internal temperature reaches 155-160 degrees. Serves 8-12.

LUAU PORK ROAST

1 (5 lb.) roast, chine bone
  removed, tied for
  roasting
3 jars strained apricots
  (baby food)
⅓ c. honey
¼ c. fresh lemon juice
¼ c. soy sauce
½ clove garlic, minced
1 small onion, minced
1 c. gingerale
⅛ tsp. ginger
⅛ tsp. pepper
1 (1 lb. 13 oz.) can whole,
  unpeeled apricots
1 Tbsp. grated lemon rind
¼ c. freshly grated
  coconut
Parsley sprigs

Place pork roast in marinating dish. Combine 2 jars strained apricots, honey, lemon juice, soy sauce, garlic, onion, gingerale, ginger and pepper; pour over pork. Marinate for 4 to 5 hours, turning occasionally. Light grill and let coals burn down until covered with grey ashes. Remove pork from marinade, reserving marinade. Place roast on a spit or in kettle-type grill. Cook over low coals for approximately 3½ hours. (Meat thermometer should register 185° when done.) During last ½ hour baste frequently with marinade. During the last 5 minutes spread 1 jar strained apricots over roast. Heat apricots and lemon rind together. Remove roast to platter. Garnish with apricots sprinkled with coconut and parsley.

GRILLED PORK TENDERLOIN

½ c. peanut oil
⅓ c. soy sauce
¼ c. red wine vinegar
3 Tbsp. lemon juice
2 Tbsp. Worcestershire
  sauce
1 clove garlic, crushed
1 Tbsp. fresh parsley,
  chopped
1 Tbsp. dry mustard
1½ tsp. pepper
2 (¾- to 1-pound) pork
  tenderloins

Combine first 9 ingredients; place in a shallow container or heavy-duty zip-top plastic bag. Add tenderloins, turning to coat. Cover or seal, and chill 4 hours, turning occasionally. Remove tenderloins from marinade. Grill, covered, 6 inches from medium coals (300 degrees to 400 degrees) for 12 to 14 minutes or until done, turning once. Yield: 6 servings.

MARINATED PORK TENDERLOIN

1 (15 oz.) can
   unsweetened sliced
   pineapple (undrained)
2 cloves garlic, minced
2 Tbsp. minced fresh
   ginger root
2 Tbsp. soy sauce
½ tsp. dry mustard
2 (¾ lb.) pork tenderloins
Vegetable cooking spray

Drain pineapple, reserving juice. Combine reserved juice and next 4 ingredients; set aside. Trim excess fat from tenderloins. Place tenderloins in a large, shallow baking dish; pour marinade over tenderloins. Cover and marinate for 24 hours in refrigerator, turning occasionally.

Coat grill rack with cooking spray. Remove tenderloins from marinade; grill over medium coals for 50 to 55 minutes, turning tenderloins occasionally. Meat is done when meat thermometer inserted in thickest part of tenderloins registers 170°. Grill pineapple slices for 5 minutes or until browned on both sides. Slice tenderloins and serve with pineapple slices.

GRILLED HAM STEAKS

4 ham slices (¾ inches
   thick)
½ c. apricot preserves
½ c. orange juice
1 Tbsp. lemon juice
1 tsp. ground ginger

Combine preserves, orange juice, lemon juice and ginger for basting sauce. Grill ham slices over hot fire for 10 minutes, basting frequently. Cut ham slices in half and serve. Serves 8.

GRILLED HAM SLICES

½ c. orange marmalade
¾ c. Dijon mustard
1 tsp. Worcestershire
   sauce
¾ c. water
6 (6- to 8-oz.) slices fully
   cooked ham, about 1
   inch thick

In a small bowl, combine marmalade, mustard, Worcestershire sauce, and water; pour into a large baking dish. Add ham slices and turn to coat. Marinate at room temperature 1 hour, or longer in refrigerator.

Prepare a medium fire. Remove ham from marinade, reserving marinade for basting. Place ham on an oiled grill set 4 to 6 inches from coals. Grill 10 to 15 minutes, turning frequently and basting with marinade during the last 5 minutes of cooking, until well browned outside and heated through.

LAMB

LAMB KABOB IN A BOWL

1 qt. meat or chicken
    broth
1 doz. French rolls
1 large (about 6 lb.) leg of
    lamb, bone-in
1 clove garlic
2 Tbsp. olive oil
1 tsp. oregano, crumbled
1 tsp. whole thyme,
    crumbled

Drill a small hole through end of shank bone. Crush garlic and blend with olive oil, oregano, and thyme. Rub this mixture over the surface of the leg of lamb.

Roast lamb slowly in a hooded barbecue; allow 2½ hours. Use a meat thermometer and roast to about 150 degrees for medium rare or 160 degrees for medium well done. Slice thinly.

Split and toast the rolls. Heat the broth. Place French roll in large soup bowl. Pour a little hot broth over roll, and place thin slices of lamb on top of broth-soaked roll. Pour desired amount of broth over meat and roll. Top with Green Pepper-Yogurt Sauce. (Recipe follows.) Serves 6 to 8.

GREEN PEPPER - YOGURT SAUCE

6 green peppers, seeded
    and cut in ½-inch-wide
    strips
6 Tbsp. olive oil
¾ tsp. liquid hot-pepper
    seasoning
6 Tbsp. flour
1 c. whipping cream
1 qt. plain yogurt
1 Tbsp. sugar

Put peppers in a bowl. Mix together the olive oil and liquid hot-pepper seasoning, and drizzle over peppers; refrigerate, covered, for 2 hours or overnight. In the top of a double boiler (or use an improvised pair of pans), blend flour with cream into a smooth paste; gradually stir in yogurt and sugar. Set over gently simmering water and heat slowly, stirring often, for 1 to 1½ hours.

Shortly before serving, turn green pepper strips and oil into a large frying pan; cook, stirring constantly, over high heat, until browned but still slightly crisp. Combine peppers and yogurt in a pan; keep warm on barbecue. Serves 6 to 8.

GRILLED LAMB STEAKS

4 shoulder lamb steaks,
  1-inch thick
½ c. red currant jelly
1 Tbsp. prepared mustard
1 Tbsp. soy sauce

Heat jelly, mustard, and soy sauce over medium heat, stirring constantly, until jelly is melted; set aside. Arrange hot briquettes for grill barbecuing. Grill steaks over medium heat until juices rise on uncooked surface. Turn steaks over and barbecue until almost done. Brush steaks several times with melted jelly during the last few minutes of barbecuing. When done, remove steaks from grill; season with salt and pepper. Allow 12 minutes per side for medium-done steaks barbecued 3 inches from briquettes.

GRILLED MARINATED LAMB STEAKS

1 (6 lb.) leg of lamb,
  boned, rolled and tied
Salt and freshly ground
  black pepper
1 large onion, thinly
  sliced
1 Tbsp. thyme
1 Tbsp. rosemary
6 sprigs fresh parsley
Rind of 1 lemon, grated
1 to 2 cloves garlic,
  minced
2 bay leaves, broken
1 c. olive oil
⅓ c. red wine vinegar

Have butcher bone the lamb, roll and tie it securely with string at four or five intervals. Using a sharp knife, cut between the strings to make four or five steaks, each one about 1½ to 2 inches thick. Place the steaks in one layer in a flat container. In a medium mixing bowl, combine the remaining ingredients and pour mixture over meat. Cover and let stand at least an hour. Grill the steaks over hot charcoal, turning carefully once or twice. Cook to desired degree of doneness. Remove the string and cut into desired number of portions.

Variation: Oregano may be substituted for the rosemary and thyme if you prefer a change in flavor.

Serves 8 to 10.

BUTTERFLIED GRILLED LEG OF LAMB

1 leg of lamb, butterflied
  by butcher
½ c. soy sauce
2 Tbsp. olive oil
Juice of 3 lemons
4 green onions, chopped
3 or 4 sprigs chopped
  fresh mint

Marinate lamb in a covered container with remaining ingredients for about 12 hours, turning meat occasionally. Barbeque meat on a charcoal grill approximately 20 minutes per side. Slice in thin strips. Lamb should be pink in the middle.

GRILLED LAMB WITH MINT

4 lb. boned lamb shoulder
or 4½ to 5 lb. boned
leg of lamb
2 cloves garlic, slivered
½ bunch (1 c.) fresh mint
leaves, chopped
1 tsp. sugar
2½ c. wine vineger
1 tsp. pepper
1 tsp. salt
2 Tbsp. olive or salad oil

Have butcher flatten lamb to 1½ inch. Wipe with damp coth, make slits, and insert garlic slivers in slits. Combine remaining ingredients; place lamb in the marinade and turn to coat well. Refrigerate, covered, several hours or overnight, turning lamb several times. Lay lamb flat on grill, fat side up; grill 17 to 20 minutes on each side, basting several times with marinade. (To cook indoors: Preheat boiler. Remove lamb from marinade, wipe with paper towels, place on rack in roasting pan and broil 4 inches from heat about 20 minutes on each side, basting several times with marinade.) Slice crosswise into ½ inch thick slices.

Serve with <u>Mint Sauce</u>: Strain ½ cup marinade; boil 15 minutes, skim surface, add ½ cup condensed beef broth and boil 5 minutes more. Add 1 tablespoon chopped fresh mint.

LAMB AND VEGETABLE KABOBS

½ c. vegetable oil
⅓ c. lemon juice
1 clove garlic, finely
chopped
2 tsp. salt
1 tsp. dried dill weed
¼ tsp. coarsely ground
pepper
1½ lb. lamb boneless
shoulder, cut into
1¼-inch cubes
4 small whole tomatoes
2 large ears corn, cut into
2-inch pieces

Mix oil, lemon juice, garlic, salt, dill weed, and pepper; pour over lamb cubes. Cover and refrigerate, turning lamb 2 or 3 times, at least 4 hours.

Remove lamb; reserve marinade. Thread lamb cubes and vegetables separately on metal skewers, leaving space between foods. Insert 2 skewers parallel and about ½ inch apart through center of tomatoes to keep them from slipping when they are turned.

Cover and grill lamb kabobs 5 to 6 inches from medium coals, turning once, until done, about 20 minutes. Cover and grill vegetable kabobs for 15 minutes, brushing 2 or 3 times with reserved marinade.

GRILLED LAMB PATTIES WITH MINT SALSA

1⅓ lb. lean ground lamb
¼ c. chopped parsley
2 Tbsp. chopped fresh
   mint, or 1½ tsp. dried
2 Tbsp. fresh lemon juice
2 garlic cloves, minced
1 tsp. salt
½ tsp. freshly ground
   pepper
Mint Salsa (recipe
   follows)

Prepare hot fire. In a large bowl, as quickly and lightly as possible, mix together lamb, parsley, mint, lemon juice, garlic, salt, and pepper until well blended. Form into 4 patties about 1 inch thick. Place patties on an oiled grill rack set 4 to 6 inches from coals and cook, turning once or twice, until well browned outside and just slightly pink in center, about 10 to 15 minutes. Serve with Mint Salsa. Serves 4.

MINT SALSA

4 large ripe tomatoes
   (about 2 lb.), seeded
   and diced
1 c. chopped onion
½ c. fresh mint leaves,
   finely chopped
2 fresh jalapeno peppers,
   seeded and minced
2 Tbsp. fresh lime juice
½ tsp. salt
⅛ tsp. freshly ground
   pepper

In a medium bowl, combine tomatoes, onion, mint, jalapenos, lime juice, salt, and pepper. Stir gently to mix. Set aside at room temperature for up to 2 hours before serving.

BARBECUED LEG OF LAMB

Leg of lamb
Fresh mint
Dry mustard
Pepper
Onion juice
¼ c. butter
½ clove garlic
1 Tbsp. onion, grated
½ c. fresh mint leaves,
   chopped
¼ c. butter

About 2 hours before cooking, cover the leg of lamb with fresh mint. Rub with dry mustard, pepper, and onion juice. While the charcoal is burning down to embers, combine the butter, garlic, and grated onion in a small saucepan on top of the stove. Cook gently for about 5 minutes. Remove the garlic, and add the chopped fresh mint leaves and butter.

Put the lamb on the grill and brush often with the warm sauce. After about 20 minutes, salt and pepper and turn the meat. Grill for 35 to 45 minutes for medium well done leg of lamb; grill for 50 to 60 minutes for well-done lamb.

FISH AND SEAFOOD

GRILLED FISH FILLETS WITH PINEAPPLE SALSA

⅓ c. seasoned rice
  vinegar
3 medium green onions,
  minced
1 (1 inch) piece fresh
  ginger, peeled and
  minced
1 tsp. Dijon mustard
4 (5 to 6 oz.) tuna steaks,
  or swordfish, red
  snapper or halibut
¾ c. fresh cilantro leaves,
  minced
Pineapple Salsa (recipe
  follows)

Mix first 4 ingredients in a large plastic bag. Add fish and seal bag tightly. Let marinate at least 30 minutes or up to 1 hour at room temperature. Prepare barbecue (high heat) preferably with a mixture of charcoal and mesquite chips.

Remove fish from bag; do not scrape off marinade. Grill fish steaks about 2½ minutes per side for medium. Transfer to plates. Spoon salsa over fish and garnish with fresh cilantro sprigs.

PINEAPPLE SALSA

½ medium pineapple,
  peeled, cored and diced
1 small red bell pepper,
  diced
3 medium green onions,
  minced
1 serrano chili, seeded
  and minced
⅛ tsp. salt
1½ piece fresh ginger,
  peeled and minced
1 Tbsp. fresh lime juice
1 clove garlic, minced

Mix all salsa ingredients, including reserved pineapple juice, in blender or food processor. Blend to a chunky consistency. Cover and let stand for at least 1 hour at room temperature. (Salsa can be prepared a day ahead and refrigerated.)

STUFFED FISH FILLETS

1 lb. fish fillets (sole,
  flounder, or halibut)
½ c. moist bread crumbs
2 Tbsp. butter or
  margarine, melted
½ c. grated carrot
1 Tbsp. green pepper,
  chopped
½ tsp. salt
Dash black pepper
Cooking oil

If fish is frozen, thaw completely before grilling. Wash fillets and pat dry with paper towels. Combine bread crumbs and next 5 ingredients in a small bowl. Toss stuffing mixture to mix well. Spread 1 or 2 tablespoons of the bread crumb mixture over each fillet. Roll up fish fillets like a jelly roll, secure with wooden picks.

Rub the hand grill with cooking oil. Put fillets in the grill and close the grill securely. Brush fillets with cooking oil and grill over medium heat until done, turning frequently and brush with more oil as required. Fish fillets held 3 inches above the hot briquettes will take about 20 minutes. Makes about 4 servings.

CHARCOAL GRILLED CATFISH

6 medium catfish
Salt and pepper
2 Tbsp. vegetable oil
6 slices bacon

Filet fish lengthwise. Salt and pepper well. Brush both sides of fish with vegetable oil, and wrap bacon around each piece of fish. Place in a wire rack and grill over charcoal fire until bacon and fish are done. Serves 6.

GRILLED TEXAS SHRIMP

¼ c. vegetable oil
¼ c. lime juice
¼ c. red wine vinegar
2 Tbsp. lime juice
1 Tbsp. ground red chiles
½ tsp. salt
2 cloves garlic, finely
  chopped
1 red bell pepper, finely
  chopped
24 large raw shrimp,
  peeled and deveined
  (leave tails intact)

Mix all ingredients except shrimp in shallow glass or plastic dish; stir in shrimp. Cover and refrigerate 1 hour.

Remove shrimp from marinade; reserve marinade. Thread 4 shrimp on each of six 8-inch metal skewers. Grill over medium coals, turning once, until pink, 2 to 3 minutes on each side.

Heat marinade to boiling in nonaluminum saucepan; reduce heat to low. Simmer uncovered until bell pepper is tender, about 5 minutes. Serve with shrimp. Serves 6.

BARBECUED SHRIMP

2½ to 3 lb. fresh or frozen
   jumbo shrimp in shells
   (36 to 42 shrimp)
1 c. olive oil or cooking
   oil
½ c. lemon juice
½ c. snipped parsley (1 c.
   lightly packed leaves)
½ c. snipped cilantro (1
   c. lightly packed leaves)
6 cloves garlic
1 Tbsp. paprika
2 tsp. ground cumin
½ tsp. ground red pepper
Salt and pepper

Thaw shrimp, if frozen. Shell and devein shrimp. Set aside.

In a blender container or food processor bowl, combine olive oil, lemon juice, parsley, cilantro, garlic, paprika, cumin, red pepper, salt and pepper. Cover and blend till finely pureed.

In a bowl, combine shrimp and puree. Cover and chill the mixture for 20 to 30 minutes. Drain shrimp, reserving marinade. Thread shrimp on skewers. Grill shrimp, on an uncovered grill, directly over medium-hot coals for about 15 minutes or just till they turn pink, turning often and brushing with marinade. Yield: 6 servings.

SEAFOOD BUTTER SAUCE AND BASTE

½ c. butter
½ tsp. rosemary
½ tsp. tarragon
¾ tsp. salt
1 Tbsp. lemon juice

Melt butter. Add remaining ingredients. Baste raw seafood before grilling and as it is grilling. As a dipping sauce, serve heated with shrimp, crawfish, crab, or lobster. Makes ½ cup.

CHARCOAL BROILED LOBSTERS

4 (1 to 1½ lb.) lobsters,
   split lengthwise
Melted butter

Drawn Butter:
½ c. butter
2 Tbsp. flour
1½ tsp. lemon juice
1 c. hot water

Open lobsters as flat as possible. Arrange hot briquettes for grilling. Lay lobsters, shell-side down, on grill; grill over medium heat about 15 minutes, brushing often with melted butter. Turn lobsters; grill about 5 minutes more. Shell is red when done. Serve with Drawn Butter. Lobsters grilled 3 inches from coals take about 20 minutes. Serves 4.

Drawn Butter: Melt ¼ cup of the butter in a saucepan; mix in flour, lemon juice and water and bring to a boil, stirring constantly. Cook and stir 5 minutes. Remove from heat; stir in remaining butter. If desired, add a few drops of yellow food coloring. Makes 1½ cups.

ORANGE-HONEY FISH

2 Tbsp. frozen orange
   juice concentrate,
   thawed
1 Tbsp. soy sauce
1 Tbsp. honey
1 Tbsp. vegetable oil
½ tsp. onion powder
1 lb. cod, haddock, or
   halibut fillets, ½ to ¾
   inch thick

Mix all ingredients except fish fillets; pour over fish in glass dish. Cover and refrigerate at least 1 hour.

Remove fish; reserve marinade. Cover and grill fish about 4 inches from medium coals, turning once and brushing 2 or 3 times with reserved marinade, until fish flakes easily with fork, 12 to 20 minutes. Cut into serving pieces if necessary. Serves 4.

SCALLOP KABOBS

1 lb. scallops
¼ lb. mushroom caps
2 Tbsp. salad oil
2 Tbsp. soy sauce
2 Tbsp. lemon juice
Onions, cut into chunks
2 Tbsp. chopped parsley
½ tsp. salt
Dash of pepper
12 slices bacon
1 (13 oz.) can pineapple
   chunks
Green pepper chunks
Melted butter

If necessary, cut scallops in bite-size pieces. Rinse. Mix oil, soy sauce, lemon juice, parsley, salt, and pepper and pour over scallops and mushrooms in shallow bowl. Cover and refrigerate 60 minutes; turn once. Partly fry bacon (or microwave). Drain; cut slices in halves. On skewers, alternate scallops wrapped in bacon, mushrooms, pineapple, green pepper, and onion. Grill 4 inches from hot coals 6 to 8 minutes on each side. Baste with butter.

To serve over rice, a good idea is to double the marinade. Marinade can be thickened with cornstarch.

SEAFOOD KABOBS

Lobster tails
Shrimp
Scallops
Cherry tomatoes or
   tomato wedges
Dill pickles
Lemon juice
Melted butter

Cook lobster tails partially in salted water for approximately 10 minutes. Cut into chunks. Parboil, peel, remove vein and leave tails on shrimp. Rinse scallops lightly. Put tomato wedges and pickles between pieces of meat on skewers, larger chunks in middle. Sprinkle with salt. Grill 10 minutes. Turn often, basting with butter (1 part lemon juice to 2 parts melted butter). Serve with tartar sauce. Sprinkle with chopped parsley.

MISCELLANEOUS SANDWICHES

GRILLED PEANUT BUTTER SANDWICH

½ c. peanut butter
¼ c. crisp bacon,
   crumbled
¼ c. sweet pickle relish
6 slices bread

Combine peanut butter, bacon, and pickle relish. Spread peanut butter mixture between slices of bread. Brush the outsides of bread with melted butter or margarine. Place the sandwich between 2 sheets of aluminum foil and grill over medium heat, turning often, until filling is very hot or melted, about 10 minutes. Yields 3 sandwiches.

SPECIAL CHICKEN SANDWICH

1½ c. minced, cooked
   chicken
⅓ c. minced celery,
   minced
⅓ c. walnuts, finely
   chopped
¼ c. mayonnaise
Salt and pepper
12 slices bread

Mix together chicken, celery, walnuts, and mayonnaise. Season to taste with salt and pepper. Spread mixture between slices of bread. Brush the outsides of bread with melted butter or margarine. Place the sandwich between 2 sheets of aluminum foil and grill over medium heat, turning often, until filling is very hot or melted, about 10 minutes. Yields 6 sandwiches.

PRAIRIE DOGS

6 hot dogs
3 slices American cheese,
   cut into halves
6 slices bacon
6 hot dog buns

Slit hot dogs, lengthwise, leaving one side hinged. Insert a thin strip of processed American cheese in slits and wrap each hot dog in a slice of bacon. Grill hot dogs over medium heat, turning several times, until bacon is done as desired. Serve in toasted buns with your favorite barbecue sauce.

NEW ENGLAND'S BEST

6 hot dogs
Mustard
Sweet pickle relish,
   drained
1 (15-oz. can) baked
   beans, drained

Slit hot dogs, lengthwise, leaving one side hinged. Spread cut surfaces with mustard; sprinkle with sweet pickle relish and fill with baked beans. Secure with wooden picks. Grill over medium heat, turning several times, until beans are hot.

GERMAN DOGS

Sauerkraut
6 hot dogs
6 hot dog buns

Drain cooked sauerkraut. Slit hot dogs, lengthwise, leaving one side hinged; fill with drained sauerkraut. Grill over medium heat; turn several times, until sauerkraut is hot. Serve in buns.

SOUTH SEA HOT DOGS

1 (12-oz. can) crushed
   pineapple, drained
6 hot dogs
6 slices bacon
6 hot dog buns

Slit hot dogs, lengthwise, leaving one side hinged. Fill each hot dog with drained pineapple and wrap in a slice of bacon; secure with wooden picks. Grill over medium heat, turning several times, until bacon is done as desired. Serve in hot dog buns.

SAUCES AND MARINADES

LEMON PEPPER THYME RUB FOR STEAKS AND BURGERS

6 Tbsp. lemon pepper
2 Tbsp. ground thyme
2 Tbsp. paprika
2 tsp. granular garlic
1 tsp. sugar
½ tsp. salt
½ tsp. MSG
¼ tsp. ground coriander
⅛ tsp. ground cumin
⅛ tsp. cayenne pepper

Mix all ingredients together with a large spoon, removing all lumps. Apply generously to steaks or burgers. Store in covered glass container. Marinate for 30 minutes or up to 2 hours before grilling. Stores for 3 to 6 months. Makes ⅝ cup.

ALL PURPOSE MARINADE

2 Tbsp. rosemary
2 Tbsp. basil
1 tsp. garlic
2 tsp. oregano
1 Tbsp. parsley

Mix all together. Keep in covered jar. Stores for 3 to 5 months. (Use 1 tablespoon with 8 ounces vinegar and oil dressing.)

BARBECUE SAUCE WITH MUSTARD

1 c. molasses
½ c. vinegar
½ c. sugar
1 c. tomato catsup
1 c. prepared mustard
2 Tbsp. canola oil
¼ Tbsp. ground oregano
½ tsp. ground thyme
1 tsp. salt
½ tsp. black pepper
⅛ tsp. red pepper (to taste)
½ tsp. cornstarch

Mix dry ingredients together. Add a little vinegar to make a paste. Mix the liquid ingredients together; add the vinegar paste. Bring all ingredients to a boil, stirring continually; simmer for 10 minutes. Let cool. Stores for 3 months in refrigerator. Makes about 4 cups.

GRILLED MEAT MARINADE

3 cloves garlic, sliced
3 Tbsp. soy sauce
2 Tbsp. ketchup
½ tsp. oregano
½ tsp. vegetable oil
Pepper to taste

Combine all ingredients. Pour over scored flank steak or a piece of meat of lesser quality that you may wish to "dress up". Chill in refrigerator several hours before grilling.

BARBECUE SAUCE

2 (14-oz.) bottles ketchup
1 (12-oz.) bottle chili
  sauce
1 Tbsp. dry mustard
⅓ c. prepared mustard
2 Tbsp. fresh ground
  pepper
1½ c. wine vinegar
1 c. fresh lemon juice
1½ c. brown sugar
½ c. bottled steak sauce
Dash of Tabasco sauce
¼ c. Worcestershire sauce
1 Tbsp. soy sauce
2 Tbsp. cooking oil
1½ c. apple cider
Minced or crushed garlic
  (optional)

Combine all ingredients. Stores for several weeks in refrigerator. May be frozen. Good with chicken or any meat. Excellent as marinade. Makes 6 pints.

CHICKEN BARBECUE SAUCE

1½ c. cooking oil
2½ c. vinegar
2 Tbsp. salt
1¼ tsp. black pepper
2½ tsp. poultry seasoning
1 tsp. red pepper
1 tsp. chili powder
⅓ c. Worcestershire sauce
Juice from 1½ lemons

Mix all ingredients. Use to baste charcoaled chicken. Makes sauce for 6 chickens (12 halves). Store in refrigerator.

MARINADE FOR CHICKEN

1½ c. cooking oil
¾ c. soy sauce
2 Tbsp. dry mustard
1 tsp. salt
½ c. wine vinegar
1½ tsp. chopped parsley
2 garlic cloves, minced
⅓ c. lemon juice
1 Tbsp. pepper

Combine all ingredients. Marinate chicken up to 24 hours.

APPETIZERS, BEVERAGES

DEVILED EGGS

6 large hard cooked eggs
2 tsp. mustard
¼ tsp. salt
Paprika
3 Tbsp. mayonnaise
1 Tbsp. vinegar
⅛ tsp. pepper

Slice eggs in halves lengthwise and carefully remove yolks. Mash yolks; add all ingredients except paprika. Spoon or pipe into egg whites. Sprinkle with paprika. Yield: 12 servings.

BASIC APPETIZER DIP

1 (8 oz.) pkg. cream cheese
Pinch of salt
1 ctn. sour cream
Pinch of onion salt
Pinch of garlic salt

Combine cream cheese, sour cream, and seasonings to blend smooth. To this basic dip may be added chili peppers, chopped shrimp, crushed nuts, crushed pineapple or mashed avocado as desired. Serve with corn chips, potato chips or crackers.

ARTICHOKE DIP

1 can or jar hearts of artichokes
1 c. mayonnaise
1 pkg. (salad) Italian seasoning

Chop artichokes and mix with remaining ingredients. Refrigerate overnight. The longer it sets, the better it tastes.

LAYERED BEAN DIP

1 (31 oz.) can refried beans
1 (4 oz.) can chopped green chilies, drained
1 (1¼ oz.) env. taco seasoning mix
2 ripe avocados, peeled and pitted
2 Tbsp. lemon juice
1 (16 oz.) jar taco sauce (mild, medium or hot), divided usage
1½ c. sour cream
3 c. shredded lettuce
1½ c. Cheddar cheese, shredded
Black olive slices

In a medium bowl, mix together refried beans, green chilies, and taco seasoning mix. Spread on a 12-inch round serving platter. Blend avocados, lemon juice, and ½ taco sauce until smooth. Spread on top of bean mixture. Spread sour cream on top of avocado mixture. Top with shredded lettuce, cheese, taco sauce, and olive slices. Serve with tortilla chips.

SPINACH DIP

1 (10 oz.) pkg. frozen leaf
  spinach
1 c. mayonnaise
1 c. sour cream
1 (8½ oz.) can water
  chestnuts, drained and
  minced
2 green onions, chopped
1 pkg. dry vegetable soup
  mix

Cook spinach and press all liquid from spinach. Mix all ingredients and chill. Best if chilled overnight. Serve in round or French bread.

POTATO SKINS

8 small baking potatoes
Garlic salt
12 slices bacon, cooked
  and crumbled
2 Tbsp. chopped green
  chiles
⅛ tsp. ground red pepper
Vegetable oil
2 c. (8 oz.) shredded
  Cheddar cheese
2 Tbsp. chopped fresh
  chives, divided
1 (8 oz.) ctn. sour cream

Scrub potatoes and rub skins with oil. Prick each potato several times with a fork. Bake at 400° for 30 to 35 minutes or until potatoes are done.

Allow potatoes to cool to touch. Cut top third off each potato; discard tops. Carefully scoop out pulp, leaving about ⅛-inch-thick shells. (Reserve potato pulp for other uses.)

Fry potato skins in hot oil (375°) for 3 to 4 minutes or until browned. Invert and drain on paper towels. Place potato skins, cut side up, on an ungreased baking sheet. Sprinkle with garlic salt and Cheddar cheese. Broil 6 inches from heat for 30 seconds or until cheese melts. Top potato skins with bacon and 1 tablespoon chives.

Press green chiles between paper towels to remove excess moisture. Combine chiles, sour cream, and red pepper in a small bowl; stir well. Top with remaining 1 tablespoon chives. Serve with potato skins. Yield: 8 servings.

BAKED STUFFED MUSHROOMS

Stuffing:
1 lb. bulk Italian sausage
1 c. diced onions
1 c. grated Parmesan
   cheese
1 tsp. chopped garlic
1 c. olive oil
2 c. dried bread crumbs

Additional ingredients:
40 medium size
   mushroom caps
Olive oil
Paprika

Stuffing: Put sausage, garlic, onions, and olive oil in a heavy saucepan. Cook on medium heat. Stir often and make sure sausage doesn't clump. When sausage is cooked, simmer for 15 minutes. Remove from heat. Stir in Parmesan cheese and bread crumbs.

Preheat oven to 450°. Spoon stuffing into mushroom caps. Arrange in baking pans. Sprinkle lightly with olive oil and dust with paprika. Bake for 15 minutes. Makes 40 appetizers.

HORS D'OEUVRES

2 (8 oz.) pkg. crescent
   rolls
8 oz. cream cheese
½ tsp. onion powder
1 tsp. dill weed
¼ head raw cauliflower,
   diced
½ green pepper, diced
6 radishes, diced
1 c. mayonnaise
½ tsp. garlic powder
3 raw carrots, grated
3 spears broccoli, diced
2 stalks celery, diced

Unroll crescent rolls and spread flat in an ungreased 10x15 inch jellyroll pan. Bake at 350° for 5 to 10 minutes or until golden brown. Cool. Leave in pan.

Blend cream cheese, mayonnaise, and seasonings. Spread on cooled crust. Vegetable pieces should be no larger than pea size. Combine vegetables and drain thoroughly. Scatter over cheese mixture. Cover with plastic wrap and gently press vegetables into cheese mixture. Refrigerate overnight and up to 3 to 4 days. Cut into squares to serve.

PINEAPPLE DIP

1 (20 oz.) can pineapple
   chunks (undrained)
1 large egg, lightly beaten
1 tsp. vanilla extract
Whole strawberries
Cantaloupe balls
¼ c. sugar
1 Tbsp. flour
1 Tbsp. butter or
   margarine
2 c. frozen whipped
   topping, thawed

Drain pineapple, reserving pineapple and ½ cup juice; set aside. Combine sugar and flour in a saucepan; add reserved pineapple juice and egg, stirring until smooth. Cook over low heat, stirring constantly, until thickened (about 4 minutes). Remove from heat; stir in butter and vanilla. Cool. Fold in topping. Serve with reserved pineapple, strawberries, and cantaloupe balls. Yields 2¼ cups.

CHERRY LEMONADE

½ c. fresh lemon juice
3¼ c. cherry-flavored
  sparkling mineral water
⅓ c. superfine sugar
Lemon slices (optional)
Fresh cherries (optional)

Combine lemon juice and sugar; stir until sugar dissolves. Cover and chill. Stir in mineral water. Serve over ice. If desired, garnish with lemon slices and cherries. Yield: 4 cups.

FROSTY PEACH PUNCH

2 (3 oz.) pkg. peach-
  flavored gelatin
2 c. boiling water
1 c. sugar
2 c. cold water
4 (.31 oz.) pkg. pink
  lemonade drink mix
2 (46 oz.) cans pineapple
  juice
1 (1-liter) bottle lemon-
  lime carbonated
  beverage, chilled

Combine gelatin, boiling water, and sugar, stirring until gelatin dissolves. Add cold water, lemonade mix, and pineapple juice, stirring until lemonade dissolves. Divide mixture into two gallon-size, heavy-duty, zip-top plastic bags. Seal and freeze.

To serve, partially thaw mixture in a punch bowl; add 1 bottle lemon-lime beverage to each bag of peach mixture. Stir gently. Yield: 2 gallons.

STRAWBERRY PUNCH

2 (28 oz.) bottles ginger
  ale, chilled
½ gal. strawberry ice
  cream, softened
1 (10 oz.) pkg.
  strawberries, thawed

Mix all ingredients together in punch bowl.

SLUSH PUNCH

2 (46 oz.) cans
  unsweetened pineapple
  juice
3 (6 oz.) cans frozen
  orange juice, thawed
2 pkg. cherry powdered
  drink mix
2 pkg. strawberry
  powdered drink mix
4 c. sugar
5 qt. water

Mix together and freeze. Take out of freezer 5 hours before serving. Chip up with fork and add 2 bottles of ginger ale.

SPICED TEA

1 large jar orange
    powdered drink mix
1½ c. sugar
2 tsp. cinnamon
½ c. lemon drink mixture
1 c. instant tea
1 tsp. ground cloves

Mix ingredients; store in a glass jar. To serve, boil water and add instant tea mix to taste. Use about 2 teaspoons to a cup.

ORANGE MINT DRINK

2½ c. water
2 c. sugar
Juice of 6 lemons or equal
    lemon concentrate
Juice of 2 to 3 oranges or
    frozen orange juice
    concentrate
2 handfuls mint leaves
Grated orange rind

Make syrup of water and sugar by boiling together for 10 minutes. Add juices and rind, then pour all over mint leaves. Cover tightly and let stand 1 hour or longer.

Strain through sieve, then through 1 thickness of cloth. Makes 1 quart concentrate, which can be kept indefinitely.

Serving instructions: Fill tall glass with finely crushed ice and ⅓ cup concentrate juice. Finish filling with cold water, ginger ale, or 7-Up.

STRAWBERRY-WATERMELON PUNCH

1 large (17 lb.)
    watermelon
1¼ c. sugar
5 c. lemon-flavored
    sparkling mineral
    water, chilled
2 c. fresh strawberries
1 c. unsweetened orange
    juice

Cut a thin slice from bottom of melon, if necessary, to prevent rolling; cut top third from other end. Scoop pulp from melon and remove seeds. Use a U-shaped knife or paring knife to make decorative cuts around edge of melon shell. Set aside. (Melon will look scalloped around the edges.)

Combine pulp and strawberries in container of an electric blender in batches; top with cover and process until pureed. Combine sugar and orange juice in a saucepan. Bring to a boil; reduce heat and simmer 5 minutes. Add to pureed watermelon mixture; cover and chill. Just before serving, stir in mineral water. Serve in watermelon shell. Yield: 5½ quarts.

SALADS

APRICOT SALAD

1 large can apricots,
drained and cut fine
(save fruit juice)
2 c. hot water
¾ c. miniature
marshmallows
1 can crushed pineapple,
drained (save fruit juice)
2 pkg. orange jello
1 c. combined fruit juices

Topping:
½ c. sugar
1 egg, beaten
3 Tbsp. flour
1 c. fruit juice
1 c. whipping cream
Grated cheese

Let jello set until halfway set; fold in fruit and marshmallows. Chill till firm.

Topping: Cook first 4 ingredients until thickened and let cool. Fold in 1 cup whipping cream, already whipped. Spread over top of thickened jello mixture. Sprinkle grated cheese over top.

BLACK BING CHERRY SALAD

1 can black cherries
1 (3 oz.) pkg. cream
cheese, broken into
small chunks
1 pkg. cherry gelatin
1 small can crushed
pineapple
1 c. cola

Heat cola to boiling (watch it as it boils over very easily). Dissolve jello in cola. While hot, add cream cheese and whip with beater. Then add 1 cup of pineapple and cherry juice (mixed). Add cherries and pineapple and chill.

CHERRY SALAD SUPREME

1 (3 oz.) pkg. raspberry
jello
1 (3 oz.) pkg. lemon jello
1 (3 oz.) pkg. cream
cheese
1 (8¾ oz.) can crushed
pineapple
1 c. finely chopped nuts
1 (21 oz.) can cherry pie
filling
⅓ c. mayonnaise
½ c. whipping cream
1 c. tiny marshmallows

Dissolve raspberry jello in 1 cup boiling water. Stir in pie filling; turn into baking dish. Chill till partially set. Dissolve lemon jello in 1 cup boiling water. Beat together cream cheese and mayonnaise. Gradually add lemon jello. Stir in the undrained pineapple. Whip the whipping cream; fold into lemon mixture with the marshmallows. Spread atop the cherry mixture and top with the nuts. Chill till set.

CUCUMBER SALAD

1 (3 oz.) pkg. lime gelatin
1 c. grated cucumbers
1 c. cottage cheese
½ tsp. salt
1 c. hot water
¼ c. chopped onions
½ c. mayonnaise

Mix gelatin with water; stir until blended. Add remaining ingredients and mix well. Refrigerate overnight in a 9x13 inch glass dish. Serves six.

This is nice because you don't have to wait for the gelatin to firm up before adding other ingredients. Quick and easy to do ahead.

HONEYDEW FRUIT BOWL

1 medium honeydew
  melon, halved and
  seeded
1 c. cubed fresh pineapple
1½ c. cantaloupe balls
1 c. fresh strawberries
⅓ c. fresh blueberries

Carefully scoop out fruit balls from honeydew halves, reserving a 1-inch thick shell. Combine honeydew balls with the next 4 ingredients; toss gently. Fill each melon half with mixed fruit. Yield: 4 to 6 servings.

TROPICAL AMBROSIA

3 large mangoes, peeled,
  cored, and cubed
2½ c. honeydew balls
1 fresh pineapple, peeled,
  cored, and cubed
½ to ¾ c. cherry syrup or
  juice
3 large papayas, peeled,
  seeded, and cubed
2½ c. watermelon balls
6 bananas, sliced
½ c. honey
Fresh mint sprig
  (optional)

Combine fruit and honey, tossing gently. Cover and chill at least 2 hours. Stir in cherry syrup or juice before serving. Garnish with a sprig of fresh mint if desired. Yield: 15 to 18 servings.

CARROT PINEAPPLE SALAD

1 can crushed pineapple,
  drained
1 large pkg. orange jello
3 carrots, grated
2 c. boiling water

Dissolve jello in boiling water. Chill until slightly thickened. Add pineapple and carrots. Chill until firm.

MANDARIN SALAD

1 medium head Bibb or
  Boston lettuce, torn
½ medium avocado,
  peeled and thinly sliced
2 green onions, thinly
  sliced
1 (11 oz.) can mandarin
  oranges, chilled and
  drained
½ c. coarsely chopped
  pecans, toasted
Freshly ground pepper to
  taste
⅓ c. commercial Italian
  dressing

Combine first 6 ingredients in a medium bowl. Add Italian dressing, tossing gently. Yield: 6 servings.

BASIC WALDORF SALAD

2 c. diced apples
1 c. chopped celery
¼ c. mayonnaise or salad
  dressing
2 Tbsp. lemon juice
½ c. walnuts
2 Tbsp. light cream

Sprinkle apples with lemon juice to keep color bright. Combine apples, celery, and walnuts. Blend mayonnaise and cream. Add to apple mixture; toss. Chill thoroughly. Serve on crisp lettuce. Yield: 6 servings.

Variations:

Add 2 cups miniature marshmallows, 1 more cup apples, and omit cream and lemon juice. Use salad dressing.

Add one 11 ounce can of mandarin orange segments.

Add 1 cup raisins or 1 cup seedless green grapes or ½ cup chopped dates or ¼ cup toasted coconut. All these varieties make for different salads.

WATERGATE SALAD

1 large can crushed
  pineapple (undrained)
1 c. pecans, chopped
1 c. miniature
  marshmallows
1 large size non-dairy
  whipped topping
1 small box pistachio
  instant pudding

Mix pudding with pineapple juice; add pineapple and non-dairy whipped topping. Add remaining ingredients and chill.

Variation: Omit pecans and marshmallows and add 2 bananas.

THREE BEAN SALAD

1 (16 oz.) can kidney
   beans
1 (16 oz.) can green
   beans
1 (16 oz.) can wax beans
1 (16 oz.) can garbanzo
   beans
1 purple onion, cut in
   rings
2 to 3 pieces celery,
   chopped
1 chopped green pepper
¾ c. sugar
½ c. oil
¾ c. vinegar
2 tsp. salt
1 tsp. pepper

Drain and rinse beans. Mix together sugar, oil, vinegar, salt, and pepper. Combine with rest of ingredients. Cover and refrigerate overnight.

KIDNEY BEAN SALAD

1 (No. 300) can kidney
   beans
2 pieces celery, sliced
2 hard cooked eggs,
   chopped
2 dill pickles, diced
¼ tsp. salt
⅛ tsp. pepper
¼ tsp. onion powder or ¼
   c. chopped onions
¼ c. mayonnaise or
   Italian dressing

Drain beans; rinse and drain again. Combine beans with celery, egg, pickle, and seasoning. Add mayonnaise or Italian dressing to taste.

MEXICAN SALAD

1 can ranch style beans
2 large tomatoes
1 lb. Longhorn cheese,
   grated
1 small bottle Catalina
   salad dressing
2 bunches small green
   onions
1 head lettuce
1 bag corn chips

Chill beans; when cold, pour beans into a bowl and rinse with water till all sauce is gone. Drain. Pour into large bowl; chop onions, lettuce, and tomatoes. Pour in with the beans. Add grated cheese. Pour dressing over salad and mix well. Refrigerate for a couple of hours. When ready to serve, crush up the bag of corn chips and stir in the salad.

CAESAR SALAD

Dressing:
¼ c. olive oil
4 tsp. fresh lemon juice
¼ tsp. freshly ground
  pepper
1 Tbsp. chopped anchovy
  fillets (optional)
1 garlic clove, minced
½ tsp. Worcestershire
  sauce

Salad:
8 c. torn romaine lettuce
½ c. grated Parmesan
  cheese
1 c. croutons
1 purple onion, sliced thin

Toss lettuce with dressing. Add onion, croutons, and cheese. Makes 6 servings.

COLE SLAW

5 c. finely chopped
  cabbage (about 1 small
  head)
½ tsp. salt
⅓ c. mayonnaise or salad
  dressing
2 carrots, scraped and
  shredded
1 to 2 Tbsp. sugar
¼ tsp. pepper

Combine cabbage and carrots in a large bowl. Sprinkle with sugar, salt, and pepper; toss gently. Stir in mayonnaise. Cover and chill thoroughly. Yield: 6 to 8 servings.

CHINESE CABBAGE SLAW

2 pkg. lightly broken
  ramen noodles without
  seasoning
½ c. oleo
1 large head cabbage
6 green onions
½ c. slivered almonds
½ c. sunflower seeds

Dressing:
⅔ c. sugar
⅔ c. oil
⅓ c. vinegar
2 Tbsp. soy sauce

Brown noodles in oleo and cool. Shred cabbage. Slice onions. Add almonds and sunflower seeds. Mix dressing and mix well. Pour over vegetables and toss. Will keep several days. Refrigerate. Serves 12.

HOT GERMAN POTATO SALAD

6 medium potatoes
¾ c. chopped onion
3 to 4 Tbsp. sugar
½ tsp. celery seed
¼ c. vinegar
6 slices bacon
2 Tbsp. flour
1½ tsp. salt
Dash of pepper
¾ c. water

Cook potatoes; cool and dice. Fry bacon; drain. Brown onions in bacon fat until lightly browned. Blend in flour, sugar, salt, celery seed, and pepper; cook over low heat until smooth and bubbly, stirring constantly. Remove from heat; stir in vinegar and water. Heat to a boil, stirring constantly. Boil 1 minute. Stir in potatoes and crumbled bacon. Yield: 6 to 8 servings.

POTATO SALAD

2½ c. sliced, cooked
    potatoes
½ c. chopped onion
1½ tsp. celery seed
2 hard-boiled eggs, sliced
1 tsp. sugar
1 tsp. vinegar
1½ tsp. salt
¾ c. mayonnaise

Sprinkle potatoes with sugar and vinegar. Add onion, seasonings, and mayonnaise; toss to mix. Carefully fold in eggs. Chill and garnish with parsley and cherry tomatoes or tomato wedges and deviled eggs. Yield: 4 servings.

TWENTY-FOUR HOUR LAYER SALAD

Cut in salad size portions:
Lettuce
Romaine
Fresh spinach

Chop and mix together:
3 whole onions
3 stalks celery
1 green pepper

Additional ingredient:
1 pkg. frozen green peas

Dressing:
¾ c. mayonnaise
2 Tbsp. wine vinegar
¾ c. sour cream
2 Tbsp. sugar

Use a 9x13 inch dish. Clean and dry spinach and lettuce; make them crisp. Begin by layering spinach, romaine, and iceberg lettuce, then sprinkle mixed vegetables. Sprinkle frozen peas on top. Pour dressing over all and sprinkle with Parmesan cheese and bacon bits. Refrigerate.

Dressing: Mix until well blended.

VEGETABLES

ASPARAGUS HOLLANDAISE

Fresh asparagus

Hollandaise Sauce:
3 egg yolks
2 Tbsp. lemon juice
1 sprig parsley
1 slice peeled onion
½ tsp. salt
⅛ tsp. pepper
½ c. butter
½ c. boiling water

Cook fresh asparagus. Add spoonful Hollandaise Sauce over each serving.

Hollandaise Sauce: Combine all ingredients, except boiling water, in glass container of mixer or blender. Blend about 5 seconds or until smooth. Add boiling water gradually as blending continues. Pour mixture into top part of double boiler. Cook over hot water, stirring briskly until sauce is consistency of soft custard. Remove from heat. Keep sauce warm over hot water until served. Or store in refrigerator and reheat over warm water when needed. Makes 1 cup sauce.

TERIYAKI VEGETABLE SHISH KABOBS

1 (15¼ oz.) can pineapple chunks, drained
8 oz. (about 2 c.) small, whole fresh mushrooms, cleaned
3 medium onions, quartered and separated into bite-size pieces
2 medium green peppers, cut into bite-size pieces
1 pt. cherry tomatoes
Zucchini or summer squash, cut into bite-size pieces

Teriyaki Marinade:
1 c. firmly packed light brown sugar
⅔ c. catsup
⅔ c. vinegar
½ c. soy sauce
½ c. vegetable oil
5 to 6 cloves garlic, finely chopped
2 tsp. ground ginger

Prepare vegetables; place all but tomatoes in large, shallow baking dish. Pour Teriyaki Marinade on top. Marinate overnight; stir occasionally. Skewer marinated ingredients with tomatoes. Grill or broil to desired doneness; brush with marinade during cooking. Makes 8 servings.

Teriyaki Marinade: In medium bowl, combine ingredients; mix well.

Tip: Teriyaki Marinade is also delicious when used to marinate pork chops or chicken.

BLACK-EYED PEAS

1¼ c. dried black-eyed
  peas
4 c. water
1 onion, chopped
1 piece salt pork or 8
  slices bacon
A little red pepper

Put all the ingredients together in a pot and cook slowly until tender, about 3 hours.

BAKED BEANS

2 large cans pork and
  beans
4 Tbsp. brown sugar
4 Tbsp. catsup
½ large onion, chopped
4 slices bacon
2 Tbsp. Worcestershire
  sauce
1 tsp. mustard or more

Combine all ingredients together. Put in casserole with bacon slices on top. Bake at 350° until bacon is well done.

OLD SETTLER'S BAKED BEANS

Brown the following:
½ lb. hamburger
1 onion
¼ lb. bacon, drained

Add and mix:
⅓ c. brown sugar
¼ c. catsup
2 Tbsp. mustard
½ tsp. chili powder
⅓ c. white sugar
¼ c. barbecue sauce
2 Tbsp. molasses
1 tsp. salt
1 tsp. pepper

Add and mix:
1 can red kidney beans,
  drained
1 can pork and beans
1 can butter beans

Bake, uncovered, for 1 hour at 350° or simmer in a crock pot.

RANCHO CALICO BEANS

½ lb. bacon (5 slices)
1 medium onion, chopped
1 (28 to 31 oz.) can pork
   and beans with tomato
   sauce or pork and
   beans with brown sugar
1 (15 oz.) can butter
   beans, drained
1 (15 oz.) can pinto
   beans, drained
½ c. packed brown sugar
½ c. catsup
2 Tbsp. vinegar
1 tsp. dry mustard
1 tsp. salt

In a skillet, cook bacon until crisp. Drain bacon, reserving 2 tablespoons drippings; crumble bacon. Cook onion in drippings till tender, but not brown. In a 3½ or 4 quart crockery cooker, combine all ingredients. Mix well. Cover. Cook on HIGH heat setting 3 to 3½ hours, uncovering for the last 30 minutes. Makes 10 to 12 servings.

May be baked in a casserole or pan, uncovered, in a 350° oven for 1¼ to 1½ hours. Stir a couple times.

Often ham is substituted for the bacon.

SPICY HOT PINTOS

1 lb. dried pinto beans
¼ lb. salt pork, cubed
1 clove garlic, minced
3 to 6 jalapeno peppers,
   seeded and chopped
2 medium tomatoes,
   peeled and diced
1 tsp. dried whole
   coriander
½ tsp. salt
3 green onions, chopped

Sort and wash beans; place in a large Dutch oven. Cover with water 2 inches above beans and bring to a boil. Cook 2 minutes. Remove pinto beans from heat; cover and let soak about 1 hour. Add salt pork and garlic to beans; cover and simmer 30 minutes. Stir in remaining ingredients; cover and simmer an additional 30 minutes or until beans are tender. Yield: 8 to 10 servings.

GREEN BEAN CASSEROLE

1 (2 lb.) can green beans,
   drained
1 can French fried onions
1 can cream of
   mushroom soup
¾ c. milk
Pepper

Combine milk, soup, and pepper and pour over beans. Add ½ can onions; pour into 1½ quart casserole dish. Bake at 350° for 20 minutes. Garnish with remaining onions. Bake 5 minutes longer. Serves 6.

ITALIAN-STYLE BROCCOLI

1½ lb. broccoli
¼ c. olive oil
1 clove garlic, peeled and
   mashed
⅓ minced, peeled onion
¼ tsp. chili powder
2 Tbsp. water
1 tsp. salt

Wash broccoli. Look over carefully. Trim stalks. Remove all large coarse leaves. Cut stalks and florets into large pieces. Heat oil in large skillet. Add garlic, onion, and chili powder. Stir and heat until onion is soft. Remove garlic and discard. Add broccoli, water, and salt. Cover skillet. Cook 12 to 15 minutes or until just tender. Serve immediately. Makes 4 servings.

BAKED CORN

1 can whole kernel corn
1 can cream corn
1 c. sour cream
1 (8½ oz.) box corn
   muffin mix
1 c. melted butter
1 beaten egg
Paprika (optional)

Mix ingredients in order given and pour into buttered 1½ quart baking dish. Bake 45 minutes at 350°.

MARINATED CARROTS

2 lb. carrots, sliced
1 onion, chopped
3 stalks celery, chopped
½ c. oil
1 Tbsp. Worcestershire
   sauce
1 can tomato soup
Salt
1 bell pepper, chopped
1 c. sugar
1 Tbsp. mustard
½ c. vinegar

Cook carrots in salted water until tender. Marinate onion, bell pepper, and celery in mixture made of the remaining ingredients. Add hot, drained carrots in marinade and refrigerate.

MUSHROOMS

1 lb. mushrooms, sliced
3 cloves garlic, minced
Butter or margarine
Salt and pepper to taste
1 onion, chopped
3 to 4 slices bacon, cut in
   fairly small pieces

In large skillet, fry bacon until almost done; add onion and garlic and saute. Add mushrooms and enough butter to cook. Add salt and pepper to taste. Cook until all vegetables are tender. Serve with grilled steak.

OKRA DELIGHT

3 Tbsp. butter or
  margarine
4 to 5 large tomatoes,
  peeled and chopped
3 c. sliced okra
2 c. fresh corn, cut from
  cob
¾ tsp. salt
¼ tsp. pepper

Melt butter in a large skillet. Stir in remaining ingredients; cover and cook over medium heat 15 minutes or until vegetables are tender. Yield: 8 to 10 servings.

FRIED GREEN TOMATOES

1 medium green tomato
  (per person)
Salt and pepper
White corn meal
Bacon drippings

Slice tomatoes about ¼ inch thick; season with salt and pepper and then coat both sides with corn meal. In a large skillet, heat enough bacon drippings to coat the bottom of the pan and fry tomatoes until lightly browned on both sides.

HASH BROWN CASSEROLE

1 (32 oz.) pkg. frozen
  hash brown potatoes
1 onion, chopped fine
1 c. sour cream
Sprinkle of pepper
Parsley flakes
1 can cream of potato
  soup
1 can cream of celery
  soup
1 bell pepper, chopped
1 tsp. salt
Paprika

Mix all ingredients, except paprika and parsley. Place in a baking dish and sprinkle with paprika and parsley. Bake 1 to 1½ hours at 350°.

NEW POTATOES WITH LEMON SAUCE

12 small new potatoes
  (unpeeled), sliced
¼ c. lemon juice
1 tsp. caper juice
2 Tbsp. chopped fresh
  parsley
¼ c. grated Parmesan
  cheese
2 Tbsp. diced onion
½ c. butter or margarine,
  melted
2 Tbsp. chopped capers
1 tsp. salt
¼ tsp. pepper
Lemon slices (optional)

Cover potatoes with water and bring to a boil; reduce heat and cook about 15 minutes or until tender. Drain potatoes; arrange slices on platter and keep warm. Saute onion in butter until tender. Reduce heat; stir in lemon juice, caper juice, capers, parsley, salt, and pepper. Cook just until mixture is thoroughly heated. Pour sauce over potatoes. Sprinkle with cheese; garnish with lemon slices if desired. Yield: 8 servings.

SUMMER GARDEN MEDLEY

¼ c. chopped onion
2 Tbsp. butter or
  margarine, melted
2 c. fresh corn, cut from
  cob
3 medium tomatoes,
  peeled and cubed
4 small yellow squash,
  sliced
1 tsp. salt
¾ tsp. dried whole
  oregano
½ tsp. sugar
¼ tsp. pepper

Saute onion in butter in a Dutch oven. Add remaining ingredients; cover and cook over medium heat 15 minutes or until the vegetables are tender. Yield: About 8 servings.

SWEET POTATO BAKE

4 sweet potatoes, sliced
¼ c. brown sugar
½ c. margarine, melted
Dash of cinnamon

Pour melted butter in baking pan. Layer sliced potatoes. Sprinkle with brown sugar and cinnamon. Bake at 350° until potatoes are tender.

BREADS

ANGEL BISCUITS

1 pkg. dry yeast
1 c. buttermilk
½ tsp. baking soda
1 tsp. salt
¼ c. warm water
2½ c. flour
1 tsp. baking powder
½ c. shortening

Dissolve yeast in ¼ cup warm water. Mix dry ingredients and cut in the shortening as in pie crust. Add yeast and buttermilk. Turn out dough on floured board and knead 10 times. Cut out biscuits. Bake on greased cookie sheet at 400° for 10 minutes.

Tip: You may use 1½ cups flour and 1 cup whole wheat.

BAKING POWDER BISCUITS

2 c. flour
3 tsp. baking powder
1 tsp. salt
⅓ c. shortening
¾ c. milk

Sift flour, baking powder, and salt together into mixing bowl. Cut shortening in with pastry blender until mixture is like coarse corn meal. Add milk, mixing lightly until dough holds together.

Start oven at hot (425°). Transfer dough to floured board. Knead lightly. Roll dough ½ inch thick. Cut into large or small rounds or other shapes with floured cutter. Bake on lightly greased cookie sheet 12 to 15 minutes, until lightly browned. Serve at once. Makes 16 to 20 biscuits.

Cheese Biscuits: Add ¼ cup grated Cheddar to dry ingredients. Complete recipe as described; sprinkle tops of biscuits on baking sheet with grated Parmesan cheese. Bake as described. Serve hot.

ITALIAN HERB BREAD STICKS

In mixing bowl, soften the yeast from one 13¾ ounce package hot roll mix in ½ cup warm water. Add flour mixture from roll mix, ½ cup dairy sour cream, 1 egg, 1 teaspoon fennel seed, and ½ teaspoon dried oregano, crushed. Mix well. Turn out on floured surface; knead 1 minute. Place in greased bowl; turn once. Cover; let rest 10 minutes. Divide into six portions. Divide each portion into 8 pieces. Roll each piece to form a pencil-like rope 12 inches long. Place on greased baking sheets. Brush with water; sprinkle lightly with coarse salt. Let rise till almost double, 20 to 30 minutes. Bake at 400° till golden brown, 10 to 12 minutes. Makes 48.

SOURDOUGH BREAD

Starter:
1¾ c. unsifted flour
1 Tbsp. sugar
1 Tbsp. salt
1 pkg. yeast
2½ c. warm water

Dough:
5 to 6 unsifted flour
3 Tbsp. sugar
1 tsp. salt
1 pkg. yeast
1 c. milk
2 Tbsp. oleo
1½ c. starter

To make starter, combine flour, sugar, salt, and dry yeast in large bowl. Gradually add warm water to dry ingredients and beat 2 minutes at medium speed. Cover and let stand at room temperature 4 days. Stir down daily.

To make dough, combine 1 cup flour, sugar, salt, and dry yeast in a large bowl. Combine milk and oleo in pan; heat over low heat until warm. Gradually add to dry ingredients. Beat 2 minutes at medium speed. Add 1½ cups starter and 1 cup flour or enough to make thick batter. Beat at high 2 minutes. Stir in additional flour to make soft dough. Turn out on floured board and knead until smooth, about 8 to 10 minutes. Place in greased bowl; cover and let rise about 1 hour, until double. Punch down and let rest 15 minutes. Shape and let rise about 1 hour. Bake at 400° for 30 minutes.

To reuse starter: Add 1½ cups warm water, ¾ cup flour, and 1½ teaspoons of sugar to unused starter. Beat 1 minute at medium speed. Cover and let stand. Stir down daily.

SWEDISH RYE BREAD

1 pkg. yeast
2 c. sifted rye flour
¼ c. brown sugar
  (optional)
1 tsp. salt
6 to 6½ c. sifted flour
½ c. warm water
½ c. dark molasses
½ c. liquid shortening
2 c. boiling water
1 egg, slightly beaten

Soften yeast in warm water. Combine rye flour, molasses, sugar, shortening, and salt. Add boiling water; stir well. Cool to lukewarm. Add softened yeast. Gradually stir in enriched flour to make a soft dough; mix well. Turn out on well floured surface. Cover; let rest for 10 minutes. Knead for 10 minutes, until dough is smooth and satiny. Place in lightly greased bowl, turning once to grease surface. Cover; let rise in warm place for 1 hour and 30 minutes, until double.

Punch down. Cover; let rise for 30 minutes, until almost double. Turn out onto a lightly floured surface and divide into 3 equal parts. Form into balls; place in greased round pans. Cover; let rise for 1 hour, until almost double. Brush loaves with egg; bake at 350° for 35 to 40 minutes. Yield: 3 loaves.

BROWN AND SERVE ROLLS

¾ c. milk
2½ tsp. salt
1 pkg. yeast
4½ c. flour
¼ c. sugar
4½ Tbsp. shortening
¾ c. lukewarm water

Scald milk; add sugar, salt, and shortening. Cool to lukewarm. Dissolve yeast in lukewarm water. Add to milk mixture. Stir in 2¼ cups flour; beat until smooth. Stir in remaining flour. Turn out on floured board. Knead lightly. Place in greased bowl. Cover with a cloth. Let rise for 1 hour and 25 minutes or until doubled. Turn out on floured board and knead. Shape into rolls; place in muffin pans. Let rise for 45 minutes. Bake at 275° to 300° for about 20 minutes; do not brown. Cool. Wrap in waxed paper. Store in refrigerator. To serve, brown at 400° for about 7 minutes.

WHOLE WHEAT BREAD OR ROLLS

1 pkg. dry yeast
1 Tbsp. sugar
3 c. unbleached flour
½ c. unprocessed bran
2 tsp. salt
¼ c. oil
½ c. warm water
4 c. whole wheat flour
½ c. wheat germ
¼ c. sugar or honey
2½ c. warm water
1 egg

Combine yeast, ½ cup warm water, and sugar in a large bowl; let stand for 20 minutes. Combine dry ingredients; add to yeast mixture with remaining ingredients. Beat until smooth, using dough hook on mixer, 10 minutes. Place dough in a greased bowl, turning to grease top. Let rise in a warm place (85°) for 1½ hours or until doubled in bulk. Turn dough out on a lightly floured surface; knead until smooth and elastic. Divide into 3 portions. Shape into loaves or rolls. Let rise until double in bulk. Bake rolls 15 minutes or loaves 30 minutes at 375°.

CORN BREAD

1 c. flour
1½ c. yellow corn meal
¼ c. sugar
2¼ tsp. baking powder
¾ tsp. salt
1 c. milk
2 eggs, slightly beaten
¼ c. oil

Preheat oven to 450°. Grease an 8 to 9 inch square pan or iron skillet. Combine all ingredients in order listed; stir until smooth. Pour batter in prepared pan. Bake 20 to 25 minutes. Batter should be creamy and pourable. If batter seems too thick, add a little more liquid.

HUSH PUPPIES

3 level c. white corn meal
4½ c. water
7 tsp. sugar
3 tsp. salt

Add salt and sugar to water. Bring water to a hard rolling boil. Meal must be warmed to room temperature while dry. Pour boiling water into warm meal and stir briskly until mixture is smooth. After mixture is cool enough to handle, roll into balls approximately one inch in diameter. Cook in deep fat fryer at 350° until golden brown. May be prepared as much as 24 hours ahead of time and cooked just before serving. Makes 3 to 4 dozen.

BLUEBERRY MUFFINS

3½ c. sifted all-purpose
   flour
2 Tbsp. baking powder
¾ c. sugar
5 eggs, slightly beaten
½ c. milk
5 oz. unsalted butter,
   melted and cooled
4 or 5 c. blueberries
   (fresh or frozen)
Additional sugar (for
   topping)
Pinch of salt (optional)

Heat oven to 425°. Mix all dry ingredients together. Stir in eggs, milk, and butter. Do not overmix. Carefully stir in blueberries. Grease the top flat surface of large muffin tins. Insert paper cups and spoon batter to the top of the paper cups. Sprinkle generously with sugar. Reduce heat to 400°; place muffin tins on middle shelf of oven. Bake about 25 minutes, until muffins are golden brown. Remove from tins; cool. Makes 15 to 16 large muffins.

APPLE NUT BREAD

½ c. oleo
2 eggs (unbeaten)
1½ Tbsp. sour cream
1 tsp. baking powder
½ tsp. salt
1 c. sugar
1 c. (medium size) apple
   (unpeeled), chopped
   fine
1 tsp. vanilla
2 c. sifted flour
1 tsp. baking soda
1 c. pecans, chopped

Cut oleo into sugar; add eggs, one at a time, mixing well after each. Blend in vanilla and sour cream. Sift together the dry ingredients; add nuts. Combine with sugar mixture. Stir in apples. Pour into greased loaf pan. Bake at 325° for 1 hour.

CHERRY DATE NUT BREAD

1 c. hot water
1 c. chopped dates
1 c. brown sugar
1 Tbsp. butter, melted
1 egg
1 tsp. vanilla
2 c. flour
1 tsp. baking powder
1 tsp. baking soda
1 c. maraschino cherries,
  chopped
½ c. chopped nuts

Pour hot water over dates. Combine brown sugar, butter, egg, vanilla, and dates in water. Sift together flour, baking soda, and baking powder; add to first mixture. Fold in cherries and nuts. Pour into 2 greased and floured 8½ x 4½ inch loaf pans. Bake at 350° for 50 to 60 minutes. Cool before slicing.

LEMON BREAD

½ c. oleo
2 eggs
1½ c. sifted flour
Dash of salt
1 c. chopped nuts
Juice of 1 lemon
1 c. sugar
Grated rind of 1 lemon
1 tsp. baking powder
½ c. milk
½ c. sifted powdered
  sugar

Cream oleo and sugar until light. Beat in eggs and rind of lemon. Sift together flour, baking powder, and salt. Add ⅓ at a time alternately with the milk to the egg and sugar mixture. Fold in nuts. Pour into an oiled loaf pan (8x4x2 inches) and bake at 350° for 45 minutes. While hot and still in the pan, put several holes in the bread with a toothpick and pour over the bread a mixture of ½ cup sifted powdered sugar and juice of lemon. Leave in pan for 10 minutes, then remove to cool with glazed side up.

STRAWBERRY BREAD

3 c. flour
1 tsp. baking soda
1 tsp. salt
3 tsp. cinnamon
2 c. sugar
2 (10 oz.) boxes frozen
  sliced strawberries,
  thawed
1 c. chopped walnuts
4 eggs, well beaten
1¼ c. oil

Sift together first 5 ingredients into a large bowl. Make a well in the center. Mix remaining ingredients and pour into the well. Stir enough to dampen all well. Bake at 350° for 45 minutes to one hour.

Flavor is better the second day. Makes 3 small or 2 large loaves. Remember to spray pans well with cooking oil spray or they stick. Halve this recipe and it makes one nice loaf.

ZUCCHINI BREAD

3 eggs
1 c. vegetable oil
1½ c. sugar
3 medium zucchini,
   grated and drained (2
   c.)
2 tsp. vanilla
2 c. sifted all-purpose
   flour
¼ tsp. baking powder
2 tsp. baking soda
3 tsp. ground cinnamon
1 tsp. salt
1 c. raisins
1 c. chopped nuts

Beat eggs lightly in a large bowl. Stir in oil, sugar, zucchini, and vanilla. Sift flour, baking powder, baking soda, cinnamon, and salt. Add to egg mixture and blend well. Stir in raisins and nuts. Spoon batter into 2 greased 8x8x3 inch loaf pans. Bake at 375° for 1 hour.

APPLE COFFEE CAKE

2 c. apples, chopped
1 Tbsp. cinnamon
1 c. sugar
1 tsp. salt
1 tsp. vanilla
½ c. chopped pecans
1 Tbsp. sugar
1½ c. sifted flour
¾ c. vegetable oil
1 tsp. soda
1 egg

Mix the tablespoon of sugar and cinnamon. Sprinkle over apples and set aside. Mix the remaining ingredients. Add apples. Bake in a greased cake pan or iron skillet at 350° for 45 minutes.

DESSERTS

FLAKY PIE CRUST

1½ c. flour
½ c. shortening, chilled
½ tsp. salt
4 to 6 Tbsp. ice water

Sift flour and salt. Cut chilled shortening into flour until shortening particles are about the size of a pea. Add just enough ice water to make a paste which will clean bowl. Roll on floured board; fold and refold the roll again. Continue this until dough is smooth. Handle quickly but gently. Makes two 8 inch crusts.

EASY PIE CRUST

1½ c. flour
1½ tsp. sugar
1 tsp. salt
½ c. salad oil
2 Tbsp. cold milk or
  evaporated milk

Mix flour, sugar, and salt in mixing bowl. Add milk to oil and stir into flour. Put mixture in 9-inch pie plate and shape.

FRENCH APPLE PIE

Unbaked 9-inch deep dish
  pie shell
⅔ c. sugar
1½ Tbsp. butter
7 c. sliced, pared apples
½ tsp. ground cinnamon

Topping:
1 c. flour
½ c. brown sugar, firmly
  packed
¼ tsp. ground cinnamon
½ c. butter

Combine apples, sugar, and cinnamon; turn into pie shell. Dot with butter; sprinkle with topping. Bake at 400° for 50 minutes or until apples are tender.

Topping: Combine flour, brown sugar, and ground cinnamon. Cut in butter until crumbly. Good with ice cream (vanilla).

BANANA CREAM PIE

½ c. sugar
¼ tsp. salt
4 Tbsp. flour
2 c. milk
2 egg yolks, slightly
  beaten
1 tsp. vanilla
2 Tbsp. margarine
2 bananas
1 (9 inch) pastry shell

Mix dry ingredients with a small amount of milk. Add remaining milk; cook over boiling water, stirring until thick. Cover and cook for 15 minutes longer, stirring occasionally. Add a small amount of the hot mixture to egg yolks. Return to hot mixture and cook a few minutes longer. Add margarine and vanilla. Slice bananas into pie shell. Pour filling over bananas. Cool slightly. Cover top of pie with meringue. Bake at 425° for 4 minutes.

BUTTERSCOTCH PIE

2 c. brown sugar
Pinch of salt
4 Tbsp. flour
3 eggs, separated
2 c. milk
1¼ tsp. vanilla
6 Tbsp. sugar
1 pie shell, baked

Combine brown sugar, salt, and flour; add yolks. Gradually add milk, stirring constantly. Cook over medium heat until thick and smooth. Cool; add ¾ teaspoon vanilla. Pour into pie shell. Combine egg whites and sugar, beating until stiff; add remaining vanilla. Spread over pie. Bake at 325° until brown. Yield: 6 servings.

RED CHERRY PIE

½ c. cherry liquid
1½ c. sugar
⅛ tsp. salt
3 Tbsp. tapioca
2 Tbsp. butter
1 tsp. lemon juice
¼ tsp. almond extract
2 (1 lb.) cans tart
    cherries, drained
Red food coloring
Pastry for 9-inch 2-crust
    pie

Combine cherry liquid, sugar, salt, and tapioca; cook until thick and clear. Add butter, lemon juice, almond extract, cherries, and enough red coloring for an appealing color. Chill; pour into pastry-lined pan. Cover with top crust. Seal edges and make vents in top crust. Bake at 425° for 45 minutes.

CHOCOLATE PIE

2 c. sugar
5 Tbsp. flour
3 Tbsp. cocoa
1 large can evaporated
    milk
1 c. water
1 stick oleo
1 tsp. vanilla
4 eggs
8 Tbsp. sugar

Separate eggs. Beat yolks slightly. Mix 2 cups sugar, flour, and cocoa. Add milk and water. Cook over medium heat until slightly thickened. Beat some of the hot mixture into egg yolks. Return to hot mixture. Cook until thick. Add oleo and vanilla. Pour into two 8 inch baked pie shells. Beat egg whites with 8 tablespoons sugar until stiff. Spread on pies and brown slightly.

CUSTARD PIE

2½ c. milk, scalded
½ c. sugar
1 tsp. vanilla
¼ tsp. salt
4 eggs, slightly beaten
1 (9-inch) pie shell

Combine milk, sugar, vanilla, and salt; mix well. Slowly stir into eggs. Pour into pie shell and bake at 400° for 20 to 25 minutes or until inserted silver knife comes out clean. Yield: 6 servings.

Note: For variation, coconut may be added or sliced bananas may be arranged in pie shell.

COCONUT CREAM PIE

4 eggs
1 c. sugar
5 (level) Tbsp. flour
1/4 tsp. salt
4 Tbsp. butter
1 tsp. vanilla
1 c. coconut
1 (9-inch) baked pie shell
1/3 c. coconut
2 c. milk

Separate eggs; put whites aside for meringue. Beat yolks in small bowl. Mix sugar, flour, and salt together in a medium saucepan. Gradually stir in milk, mixing well. Cook for 2 minutes. Remove from heat; stir small amount of hot mixture into slightly beaten egg yolks; immediately return to hot mixture. Cook another 2 minutes, stirring constantly. Remove from heat; stir in butter, vanilla, and coconut. Pour into baked pie shell. Beat egg whites with 1/2 teaspoon vanilla and 1/4 teaspoon cream of tartar till soft peaks form. Gradually add 6 tablespoons sugar, beating till stiff peaks form and all sugar is dissolved. Spread atop pie. Sprinkle with 1/3 cup coconut. Bake at 350° for 12 to 15 minutes or until meringue is golden brown.

ICE CREAM PIE

1/4 c. brown sugar
1 c. flour
1/2 c. nuts, chopped finely
1/2 bottle caramel topping
1/2 c. oleo
1 qt. vanilla ice milk,
   softened

Mix sugar, flour, nuts, and melted oleo. Spread thin on greased cookie sheet, mashing flat and thin. Bake at 400° for 15 minutes. Crumble into bowl with fork while still hot. Spread thin layer of crumbles over bottom of buttered pie pan. Spread ice cream on top of crust. String topping over ice cream. Sprinkle more crumb mixture on top. Freeze. Makes 2 pies.

LEMON MERINGUE PIE

1 c. sugar
3 Tbsp. cornstarch
1 1/2 c. cold water
3 egg yolks, slightly
   beaten
1 Tbsp. butter
1/4 c. lemon juice
Grated rind of 1 lemon
1 (9-inch) baked pastry
   shell

Meringue:
3 egg whites
1/3 c. sugar

In 2 quart saucepan, stir together 1 cup sugar and cornstarch. Gradually stir in water until smooth. Stir in egg yolks. Stirring constantly, bring to boil over medium heat and boil 1 minute. Remove from heat. Stir in next 3 ingredients. Cool. Turn into pastry shell.

In small bowl with mixer at high speed, beat egg whites until foamy. Gradually beat in 1/3 cup sugar; continue beating until stiff peaks form. Spread some meringue around edge of filling first, touching crust all around, then fill in center. Bake in 350° oven for 15 to 20 minutes or until lightly browned. Cool. Serves 6 to 8.

PEACH PIE

Filling:
4 c. fresh, sliced peaches
2 Tbsp. flour
¼ tsp. salt
1 c. sour cream
1 c. sugar, divided
1 egg
½ tsp. vanilla

Crust:
½ c. butter
1½ c. flour
½ tsp. salt

Topping:
⅓ c. sugar
¼ c. butter
⅓ c. flour
1 tsp. cinnamon

Crust: Cut butter into flour and salt. Press dough into 9-inch pie pan.

Filling: Slice peaches into a bowl; sprinkle with ¼ cup sugar. Let stand while preparing rest of filling. Combine ¾ cup sugar, flour, egg, salt, and vanilla. Fold in sour cream. Stir into peaches. Pour into crust. This pie is best baked at two different temperatures. Set your oven at 400° and bake for 15 minutes, then bake at 350° for 20 minutes.

Make topping by combining sugar, cinnamon, flour, and butter until crumbly. Sprinkle crumbs evenly over pie and bake for 10 minutes at 400°.

RHUBARB PIE

3 c. rhubarb
2 Tbsp. flour
Juice of ½ lemon
2 Tbsp. butter
1 c. sugar
1 egg, beaten
Pastry for two-crust pie

Cut rhubarb into 1-inch pieces; add sugar, flour, egg, and lemon juice. Turn mixture into pie shell and dot top with butter. Add top pastry and sprinkle with additional sugar. Bake for 40 minutes at 400°.

FRENCH STRAWBERRY PIE

1 baked 9-inch pie shell
1 (3 oz.) pkg. cream
  cheese
3 Tbsp. cream
1 qt. strawberries
1 c. sugar
1 c. whipping cream
2 Tbsp. cornstarch
Few drops of lemon juice

Blend cream cheese and cream until soft and smooth. Spread over the cooled pie shell. Wash and hull the berries. Select one half of the best ones. If they are large, slice in halves. Add the sugar to the rest and let stand until juicy. Mash and rub through a sieve. Mix this puree with the cornstarch. Add a few drops of lemon juice. Cook this mixture until thick and transparent, stirring constantly. Cool and put half over the cream cheese. Arrange the berries in the sauce and then pour the remaining puree over the berries and chill. To serve, top with sweetened whipped cream.

PEACH COBBLER

3 c. peaches
1/4 c. sugar
1 tsp. almond extract
1 Tbsp. lemon juice
1 Tbsp. sugar
1/3 c. shortening
1 1/2 c. flour
3 tsp. baking powder
1/2 tsp. salt
1 egg, beaten
2 Tbsp. sugar

Grease 8 inch square dish. Sprinkle sugar, almond extract, and lemon juice over peaches plus 1 tablespoon sugar. Cut shortening into flour, salt and baking powder until like coarse crumbs. Add egg and enough milk until flour is moistened. Spread over peaches. Sprinkle with sugar. Bake at 375° for 30 minutes.

CHERRY DESSERT

1 1/2 c. flour
2 Tbsp. sugar
1 c. chopped pecans
3/4 c. oleo
1 (8 oz.) pkg. cream cheese
2 c. powdered sugar
2 env. instant whipped topping
1 (22 oz.) can cherry pie filling

Mix well the flour, sugar, pecans, and oleo. Press into bottom of a 13x9 inch pan. Bake at 350° for 20 minutes or until light brown. Soften cream cheese to room temperature and cream with powdered sugar. Prepare instant whipped topping according to package directions and blend into cream cheese mixture. Spread over cooled crust. Pour pie filling over the top. Chill well.

LEMON SQUARES

2 c. flour
2 sticks margarine
1/4 tsp. salt
1/2 c. powdered sugar
4 eggs
2 c. sugar
4 Tbsp. flour
7 Tbsp. lemon juice (fresh)

Combine first 4 ingredients until well blended. Press into 9x13 inch pan. Bake at 350° for 20 minutes. Mix last 4 ingredients (eggs, sugar, flour, and lemon juice) with wire wisp. Pour onto crust. Bake 20 minutes. Sift powdered sugar over top while warm.

OLD-FASHIONED VANILLA ICE CREAM

4 eggs
2 1/4 c. sugar
5 c. milk
4 c. cream
4 1/2 tsp. vanilla
1/2 tsp. salt

Add sugar gradually to beaten eggs. Continue to beat until mixture is very stiff. Add remaining ingredients and mix thoroughly. Pour into gallon freezer and freeze as directed.

FRUIT PIZZA

1 regular pkg. refrigerated
  sugar cookie dough
1 (8 oz.) pkg. cream
  cheese
1/3 c. sugar
1 tsp. vanilla
Fruits such as kiwi,
  strawberries, peaches,
  bananas, blueberries,
  raspberries, etc.

Slice cold cookie dough into 1/8 inch slices and place over pizza pan. Press dough to cover pan. Bake at 350° for 12-15 minutes until golden brown. Cool.

Mix together cream cheese, sugar and vanilla. Spread on cookie dough. Arrange fruit in circular pattern. Refrigerate.

Peaches and bananas can be dipped in lemon juice to prevent browning.

STRAWBERRY SHORTCAKE

Shortcake (see recipe
  below)
1 c. whipping cream
Butter or margarine,
  softened
3 to 4 c. sweetened,
  halved strawberries

Shortcake:
2 c. all-purpose flour
1 Tbsp. baking powder
1/2 c. butter or margarine
2/3 c. light cream
2 Tbsp. sugar
1/2 tsp. salt
1 beaten egg

Prepare and bake shortcake in 8 x 1½-inch round baking pan; remove from pan and cool on rack about 5 minutes. Using a sharp knife, gently split shortcake horizontally into two layers; lift off top carefully. Place bottom layer on serving plate. Spread a little softened butter over bottom layer.

In chilled bowl, whip cream to soft peaks (tips curl over). Spoon half of the strawberries and the whipped cream over bottom cake layer. Top with second layer. Spoon remaining strawberries and whipped cream over the top. Serve while cake is still warm. Makes 6 to 8 servings.

Shortcake: In mixing bowl, stir together the flour, sugar, baking powder, and salt. Cut in the butter till mixture resembles coarse crumbs. Combine the egg and light cream; add all at once to flour mixture, stirring with fork just to moisten. Spread dough in greased 8 x 1½-inch round baking pan or a greased 8 x 8 x 2-inch baking pan, building up edges slightly. Bake in a 450° oven for 15 to 18 minutes or till done. Remove from pan and cool slightly.

ANGEL FOOD CAKE

1½ c. egg whites
¼ tsp. salt
2 level tsp. cream of
   tartar
1⅝ c. sugar
1 c. sifted cake flour
½ tsp. almond extract
1½ tsp. vanilla

Start oven at moderate (375°). Have ready 10x4-inch tube pan; do not grease pan. Sift flour and ¾ cup sugar together 3 times. Separate eggs carefully. Drain off whites into measuring cup to make 1½ cups egg whites. Let stand at room temperature 15 minutes or longer. Beat whites with cream of tartar and salt in mixing bowl or in electric mixer until frothy. Beat in remaining sugar, ¾ cup plus 2 tablespoons, a little at a time, beating for 10 seconds after each addition, using medium speed on mixer. Continue beating, now at high speed on mixer, until meringue is firm and holds stiff points when whip is pulled out. Fold in flavorings.

Sift flour-sugar mixture, about 3 tablespoons at a time, over meringue. Cut and fold gently with wire whip until flour-sugar mixture disappears each time. Use rubber scraper and push batter from mixing bowl into tube pan. Spread and level batter against tube and sides of pan. Cut through batter gently with a knife. Bake 30 to 35 minutes or until no imprint remains when finger lightly touches top of cake. Invert cake immediately, placing tube over upturned funnel on kitchen table. Let hang until cold. Remove cake from pan. Frost as preferred. Makes 8 or more servings.

BANANA SPLIT CAKE

2 c. graham cracker
   crumbs
1 lb. powdered sugar
2 sticks oleo, softened
1 large can crushed
   pineapple, drained
1 c. chopped maraschino
   cherries
1 stick oleo
2 eggs
5 bananas
1 large container non-
   dairy whipped topping
1 c. chopped nuts

Melt 1 stick oleo in 9x13 inch pan. Add cracker crumbs. Mix and pat over bottom of pan. Mix sugar, eggs, and 2 sticks oleo and beat for 15 minutes. Pour over crust. Slice bananas and arrange on top of filling. Top with pineapple. Spread non-dairy whipped topping on top of pineapple. Sprinkle with nuts and cherries. Cover and refrigerate overnight.

CARROT CAKE

For cake:
1½ c. oil
2 c. sugar
2 c. grated carrots
4 eggs
2 c. flour
2 tsp. cinnamon
2 tsp. soda
1 tsp. salt

For icing:
1 (8 oz.) pkg. cream
  cheese
1 stick oleo
1 box powdered sugar
1 tsp. vanilla
1 can *well drained*
  crushed pineapple

Cake: Cream oil and sugar together; add carrots. Add eggs one at a time, then stir in dry ingredients. Pour into 3 buttered layer pans and bake at 350° for 25 to 30 minutes.

Icing: Cream the cheese and oleo together. Add sugar and vanilla, then crushed pineapple. Spread between layers and over cooled cake.

CARAMEL CRUNCH FUDGE CAKE

½ c. margarine or butter
2 oz. (2 sq.) unsweetened
  chocolate
1 c. water
1 c. rolled oats
1 c. sugar
1 c. firmly packed brown
  sugar
½ c. chocolate-flavored
  syrup
½ c. coffee
1 tsp. vanilla
3 eggs
1½ c. all-purpose flour
1 tsp. baking soda
½ tsp. salt

Topping:
⅓ c. margarine or butter
¼ c. whipping cream
¾ c. firmly packed brown
  sugar
½ c. coarsely chopped
  nuts

Heat oven to 350°. Grease 13x9 inch pan. In large saucepan, melt margarine and chocolate. Add water; bring to a boil. Stir in oats, sugar, brown sugar, chocolate syrup, coffee, vanilla, and eggs; mix well. Stir flour, baking soda, and salt into chocolate mixture, mixing well. Pour into greased pan. Bake at 350° for 25 to 30 minutes or until cake springs back when touched lightly in center.

As soon as cake is removed from oven, in small saucepan, combine all topping ingredients. Bring to a boil over medium heat, stirring constantly. Reduce heat; simmer 2 to 3 minutes or until slightly thickened. Pour over hot cake. Broil 4 to 6 inches from heat for about 2 minutes or until topping is bubbly and lightly browned. Makes 12 servings.

DUMP CAKE

20 oz. crushed pineapple
  (undrained)
20 oz. cherry pie filling
  (or apple or blueberry)
1 box yellow cake mix
1 c. nuts
1 c. melted oleo

Dump all ingredients in a 9x13 inch pan. Do not stir or mix. Spread a few extra nuts on top. Bake at 350° for ½ hour.

GERMAN CHOCOLATE CAKE

1 (4 oz.) German's sweet
  chocolate
½ c. boiling water
1 c. butter or margarine
2 c. sugar
4 egg yolks (unbeaten)
1 tsp. vanilla
2½ c. sifted cake flour
½ tsp. salt
1 tsp. soda
1 c. buttermilk
4 egg whites, stiffly
  beaten

Melt chocolate in boiling water; cool. Cream butter and sugar until fluffy. Add egg yolks, one at a time; beat well. Add chocolate and vanilla; mix well. Sift flour, salt, and soda together. Add alternately with buttermilk to chocolate mixture; beat until smooth. Fold in egg whites. Pour into three deep 8 or 9 inch waxed paper-lined pans. Bake at 350° for 30 to 40 minutes. Cool.

COCONUT-PECAN FROSTING

1½ c. evaporated milk
4 egg yolks
1½ tsp. vanilla
1½ c. sugar
¾ c. butter or margarine
2 c. coconut
1½ c. chopped pecans

Combine milk, sugar, egg yolks, butter, and vanilla in a heavy saucepan. Cook over medium heat, stirring constantly, until mixture thickens. Remove from heat. Add coconut and pecans. Beat until cool and of spreading consistency. Makes 4¼ cups.

GERMAN CHOCOLATE POUND CAKE

1 bar German's sweet
  chocolate
2 c. sugar
1 c. shortening
4 eggs
2 tsp. vanilla
2 tsp. butter flavoring
1 c. buttermilk
3 c. sifted all-purpose
  flour
½ tsp. soda
1 tsp. salt

Partially melt chocolate over hot water. Remove and stir rapidly until melted. Cool. Cream sugar and shortening. Add eggs, flavoring, and buttermilk. Mix well. Sift together flour, soda, and salt; add to shortening mixture. Stir well. Blend in chocolate. Pour into greased and floured 9 inch tube pan. Bake in slow oven for about 1½ hours. Remove from pan while still hot.

SCRUMPTIOUS LEMON CAKE

8 egg yolks
1¼ c. sugar
2½ c. sifted cake flour
¼ tsp. salt
1 tsp. grated lemon rind
1 tsp. vanilla extract
¾ c. butter or margarine,
    softened
1 Tbsp. baking powder
¾ c. milk
1 tsp. fresh lemon juice
Lemon Frosting

Garnishes:
Lemon wedges
Fresh mint leaves

Lemon Frosting:
1 c. butter or margarine,
    softened
2 tsp. grated lemon rind
⅓ c. lemon juice
8 c. sifted powdered sugar
1 to 2 Tbsp. half & half
    (optional)

Beat egg yolks at high speed with an electric mixer 4 minutes or until thick and pale. Set aside.

Beat butter at medium speed with an electric mixer until creamy; gradually add sugar, beating well. Add egg yolks, beating well.

Combine flour, baking powder, and salt; add to butter mixture alternately with milk, beginning and ending with flour mixture. Mix after each addition. Stir in lemon rind, juice, and vanilla. Pour in three 8 or 9 inch well greased and floured pans. Bake at 350° for 30 to 35 minutes. Test with toothpick.

Spoon about 1 cup Lemon Frosting into a decorating bag fitted with a large tip; set aside. Spread remaining frosting between layers and on top and sides of cake. Pipe 8 frosting rosettes around top edge of cake and garnish if desired. Chill until serving time. Yield: One 3 layer cake.

Lemon Frosting: Beat butter at medium speed with an electric mixer until creamy; stir in lemon rind and juice. (Mixture will appear curdled.) Gradually add sugar; beat at high speed 4 minutes or until spreading consistency. Gradually add half & half if needed. Yield: 4 cups.

ORANGE PINEAPPLE CAKE

1 box yellow cake mix
1 can mandarin oranges
    (juice included)
1 large can crushed
    pineapple
1 small box vanilla
    instant pudding
1 c. oil
4 eggs
1 large container non-
    dairy whipped topping

Mix well the cake mix, oranges, oil, and eggs. Pour into 3 layer pans. Bake at 350° for 35 to 40 minutes. Drain large can pineapple, reserving juice. Pour juice over cake layers while they are still hot. Let cool. Mix non-dairy whipped topping with pineapple and pudding. Beat well. Ice layers with mixture. Refrigerate.

PINEAPPLE UPSIDE-DOWN CAKE

Fruit Topping:
1/2 c. butter or oleo
1 c. scant brown sugar
1/2 tsp. cinnamon
1 (8 oz.) can pineapple
 slices
1/2 c. nut halves

Batter:
1/2 c. butter
1 c. sugar
2 eggs
2 c. flour
2 tsp. baking powder
1/2 tsp. salt
1 c. milk
1 tsp. vanilla

Fruit Topping: Heat butter, sugar, and cinnamon on bottom of a 10 inch cast iron skillet until sugar is melted. Arrange pineapple slices, whole or halved, with nuts in skillet.

Batter: Beat butter; add sugar. Cream till light. Beat in eggs, one at a time. Measure dry ingredients and mix. Add to butter mixture alternately with milk, beginning and ending with flour. Stir in vanilla. Pour over topping in skillet. Bake at 350° till cake is done. Test with toothpick. Invert cake onto plate.

BUTTERSCOTCH-MOCHA POUND CAKE

1 (6 oz.) pkg.
 butterscotch flavored
 morsels
1/4 c. water
1 1/2 c. sugar
3 c. all-purpose flour
1/4 tsp. salt
4 eggs
2 Tbsp. instant coffee
 powder
1 c. butter or margarine,
 softened
1/2 tsp. soda
3/4 c. buttermilk

Combine butterscotch morsels, coffee powder, and water in top of a double boiler; place over boiling water and stir until smooth. Set aside.

Combine butter and sugar; cream until light and fluffy. Stir in butterscotch mixture. Combine flour, soda, and salt; add to creamed mixture alternately with buttermilk, beating well after each addition. Add eggs, one at a time, beating well after each addition. Pour batter into a well greased and floured 10-inch Bundt pan. Bake at 350° for 55 to 60 minutes. Cool 10 minutes; remove from pan.

ORANGE GLAZED PUMPKIN CAKE

Cake:
2 c. firmly packed brown
　sugar
¾ c. butter flavored
　shortening
1 (16 oz.) can solid pack
　pumpkin or 16 oz. fresh
　cooked pumpkin
4 eggs
¼ c. water
2 c. all-purpose flour
1⅓ c. oats (uncooked)
½ to 1 c. chopped nuts
　and raisins
4 tsp. baking powder
1 Tbsp. pumpkin pie spice
1½ tsp. baking soda
¾ tsp. salt

Glaze:
1 c. powdered sugar
4 tsp. orange juice
¾ tsp. grated orange peel

Heat oven to 350°. Grease a 10 inch Bundt or tube pan. For cake, beat sugar and shortening till fluffy. Mix in pumpkin, eggs, and water. Combine remaining cake ingredients and mix well. Gradually add to pumpkin mixture while mixing well. Spread mixture into pan. Bake 60 to 70 minutes or until toothpick comes out clean. Cool for 10 minutes. Remove from pan. Cool completely on a wire rack. Makes 16 servings.

For glaze, mix all ingredients until smooth, then drizzle over the cake.

RASPBERRY ALMOND TORTE

Torte:
1 c. whole blanched
　almonds
⅓ c. flour
½ tsp. baking powder
¾ c. sugar
¼ c. melted butter
3 eggs
2 tsp. vanilla
¼ tsp. almond extract
1 Tbsp. grated lemon peel

Glaze:
⅓ c. sugar
¼ c. lemon juice

Line 9 inch round pan with waxed paper. Grease and dust with flour. Grind almonds finely in blender or processor. Add flour and baking powder. In mixing bowl, combine sugar, butter, eggs, extracts, and lemon peel. Stir in almond-flour mixture. Pour into pan. Bake at 300° for 35 to 40 minutes. Loosen edges to turn onto serving plate.

Glaze: Bring ⅓ cup sugar and ¼ cup lemon juice to a boil. Pour onto torte and let set.

To serve: Spread ¾ cup raspberry preserves on top of entire torte or large dollop per wedge. Garnish with whipped cream or ice cream and top with sliced almonds.

INDEX OF RECIPES